The
New Yankee
Workshop

The
New Yankee
Workshop

by Norm Abram

with Tim Snyder

Little, Brown and Company
Boston   Toronto   London

First Edition

Design and production-Barbara Snyder
Illustrations-David Dann
Black and white photos-Tim Snyder
Color process photos-Tim Snyder, Russ Morash
Chapter opening photos-Paul Ross,Russ Morash
Typesetting-Batsch/Spectra Comp

Library of Congress Catalog Card Number 88-83986

HC: 10   9   8   7   6   5   4   3   2   1
PB: 10   9   8   7   6   5   4   3   2   1

Published simultaneously in Canada by
Little, Brown and Company (Canada) Limited
Printed in the United States of America

684   1. Woodwork
       2. Cabinet work.

E

Contents

I dedicate this book to my father, who taught me patience, persistence and the skills necessary for carpentry and woodworking. I now share these rewarding skills with others.

Foreword

I first met Norm Abram one day in 1968 when an architect friend introduced us. Norm was framing a new house for my friend on Nantucket Island and I was invited over to meet the impressive man who was doing the job all by himself. "Wait till you see the size of his trim pile," my friend exclaimed. "He wastes nothing." This turned out to be true. Norm was building a fairly complicated structure with lots of fancy cuts, yet nowhere could I see a cut-off longer than four inches.

You don't meet such a craftsman every day: working alone, conserving resources, producing first-rate results. It didn't take me long to offer Norm a job. I needed a garage-workshop built. If I was to take care of the foundation, could he frame it and complete the exterior? "It's possible," he mumbled, in the manner of those who've learned to keep things flexible. "I've got some work ahead of you." I never thought I'd see Norm again.

A month later, just as the winter weather settled in, Norm arrived to begin my project. He came alone every cold day at dawn and built the structure we had agreed to: without overruns, without delays, without incidents. Only once was I able to give him any help, when it seemed he might be crushed by the incredibly heavy main steel beam that had to be raised in place. Norm had already lifted a slightly smaller piece into position without help, and I suspect he would have found a way to do so with this heavier one when I happened on the scene. I was impressed.

A few months later I was trying to bring a new series of television programs to PBS. The idea was to find an old house and fix it up. Each week, the program would show progress, introduce the craftsmen and show viewers, step-by-step, how to tackle various projects. Bob Vila was to be host of *This Old House*, acting as the glue to hold the various elements together. But to actually do the work and serve as general contractor we turned to my new friend Norm Abram.

I have fond memories of that first *This Old House* project, but none more vivid than seeing Norm hanging from the eaves, freezing rain dripping on him from the rotting roof, as he patiently explained to Bob Vila and millions of viewers that the decay was worse than anyone had imagined. As I looked at Norm's worried wet face through my TV monitor, it occurred to me that we were in deep trouble. How could we possibly save this old relic, in full view of the public, in a finite number of programs, and within our limited budget? The answer, of course, was standing there on the soggy scaffold. Norm would do it.

In the years since *This Old House* began, Norm has proved again and again that he is not only a gifted craftsman but a great teacher as well. It is not as easy as he makes it look to discuss a complex building technique while performing a task at the same time. As the series progressed from season to season, viewers particularly responded to the scenes that featured Norm in his TV workshop, building various projects, such as bathroom vanities, bookcase units, and kitchen cabinets. These segments highlighted Norm's special genius for achieving high-quality craftsmanship and joinery techniques using a selection of hand and power tools and the professional tips and shortcuts gained through his own experience.

It was our literary agent, Don Cutler, who proposed the idea for a book by Norm Abram, one that would focus on his cabinetmaking skills. We envisioned a book that would take readers step-by-step through the process of building handsome, useful pieces of furniture, inspired by the classic Shaker designs we found at Old Sturbridge Village, Hancock Shaker Village, and the Fruitlands Museums. The clean lines, pleasing proportions, and superbly fashioned mortise-and-tenon joinery seemed perfectly suited to Norm's approach to the craft: traditional techniques accomplished with modern woodworking equipment and basic skills. Thus *The New Yankee Workshop* was conceived.

Such a book demanded numerous illustrations and photographs. We imagined that Norm would actually build each piece of furniture while a photographer stood by to record the action. However, this seemed guaranteed to break the photography budget, so we decided instead to provide continuous electronic coverage using a small home video camera and a single cameraman. This modus operandi coincided with WGBH's urgent demand for more home videos to follow on the heels of the very successful one we'd done starring Norm and Bob Vila. In a stroke of serendipity, we expanded our vision of the New Yankee Workshop to include Norm's book, the home videos, and a full-fledged PBS series.

The constraints of our budget have kept Norm, in his stardom, quite close to his frugal beginnings: he is surely the only television celebrity to have built his own studio. But then, who could have done a better job of building the New Yankee Workshop? It's a wonderful place, full of things dear to the hearts of woodworkers: the tools, the lumber, the books on furniture design, the patterns hanging on the wall. Its character is all Norm's. He is the "new Yankee," the smart craftsman who knows what works and what doesn't. If he says it, you can depend on it. Norm always measures twice.

Executive Producer, WGBH Television

Acknowledgments

This book could not have taken form without the efforts of many people, those behind the scenes as well as the more visible participants. Russell Morash is the visionary behind *The New Yankee Workshop*, as he has been for *This Old House*. He got me into all of this, and I'm grateful to him—most of the time! David Liroff, station manager at WGBH Educational Foundation, believed in this project from the start. Associate producer Nina Sing provided indispensable help with the research and all the production details at every step of the way. Tim Snyder worked side by side with me to capture each of the woodworking projects in clear text and photos of the process. Marian Morash paid bills and sustained us with wonderful lunches. Barbara Snyder designed the book, giving form to its substance. David Dann produced the handsome drawings showing details of each project's construction. Paul Ross took the photographs for the chapter openers. Kate Morash helped with them. Ed Rawson allowed us to photograph his trestle table and blanket chest at his home on Nantucket. Lynne Wilson and Carol Snell graciously lent us their homes for photographing some of the other pieces. Adam Cohen and Derrick Diggins applied both brains and brawn to the job of building the workshop. Lisa DeFrancis designed our logo. At Little, Brown and Company, William D. Phillips has been this book's guiding light through the publication process. Christina Ward kept the communication lines humming and the many pieces and participants together. Nan Nagy and Ellen Bedell worked miracles in book production. Don Cutler, our steadfast literary agent, has kept the faith and, once again, moved mountains with it.

Special thanks go to our series underwriters, the Parks Corporation, makers of Carver Tripp wood finishing products, and the Square D Company, makers of electrical distribution and control equipment. Without their support, *The New Yankee Workshop* would still be a gleam in Russ Morash's eye.

Perhaps our greatest debt of all is to the anonymous craftsmen whose work lives on in places like Old Sturbridge Village, the Hancock Shaker Village, and Fruitlands Museums. Their enduring artistry and skill have inspired both the designs and the techniques at the heart of the New Yankee Workshop.

The
New Yankee
Workshop

Introduction

Setting up shop

As the name suggests, there's something new and something old about the New Yankee Workshop. Here at the workshop, we'll continue the heritage of woodworking craftsmanship that has given us such a wealth of fine furniture to study, enjoy and inspire our own furniture-building efforts. The idea behind the New Yankee Workshop is to build traditional-style furniture using modern tools, materials and techniques. Woodworkers of earlier generations did all their work by hand, shaping joints and straightening wood with sharp saws, chisels and hand planes. Today power tools make it possible to do the same work with greater speed and accuracy. With a basic selection of power and hand tools, we can build furniture pieces today that will become heirlooms in years ahead..

Once we're done setting up shop, you'll find that each chapter is devoted to building a piece of furniture from start to finish. You can duplicate the piece that I've made, or change the dimensions or the type of wood used to suit your taste. Refer to the "Project planning" box near the beginning of each chapter for information about special tools, materials and project guidelines. The last chapter, on finishing, is where you can learn about techniques and options for painting, staining or varnishing your furniture. There's also information about sanding and surface preparation, so it's a good idea to look this chapter over before you start to build. No matter which piece you build first, take your time. Be patient when you're trying out new techniques, work safely and enjoy making each joint.

The inspiration of Shaker style

Many of the furniture pieces in this book are direct descendants of authentic Shaker furniture that you'll find in homes, museums and antique stores. A tightly knit religious society, the Shakers came to the United States in the late 1700s and established small, largely self-sufficient communities where they devoted themselves to worship and work.

Frugal and industrious, the Shakers became well known for achievements in horticulture and animal husbandry as well as in woodworking. A Shaker cupboard or table stands out because of its simple lines, pleasing proportions and purposeful design. Ornamentation is traditionally subdued if it exists at all, and the joinery work is first-class.

Rather than attempt to build exact replicas of Shaker originals for this book, I've used traditional Shaker style as an inspiration for my own designs. Some pieces, like the bedside table (chapter 5) and candle stand (chapter 10), are nearly identical to their antique counterparts. Other pieces, like the medicine cabinet (chapter 1) and bathroom vanity (chapter 6), embody the traditional joinery and functional design that we've come to associate with Shaker style.

Joinery details and woodworking jargon

Before talking about the tools I'll be using in the New Yankee Workshop, we should go over some of the terminology that relates to joinery details and woodworking operations in general. Interestingly enough, most of our woodworking vocabulary has changed little since the first Colonial woodworkers came to ply their trade in the New World. The joinery details that we'll use in the New Yankee Workshop are identical to those used by early furniture makers. It's mostly the joint-making techniques that have changed, thanks to power tools.

Have a look at the basic selection of wood-to-wood joints shown here. We'll be using these joints, and variations of them, throughout the book. The most important joint in making traditional-style furniture is the mortise-and-tenon joint. I'll be cutting (also called "milling") mortise-and-tenon joints in nearly every project, so we should take a closer look at the mortise and tenon to get a good idea of its anatomy. "Shoulders," "cheeks," and other details are shown in the mortise-and-tenon drawing.

Basic woodworking joints

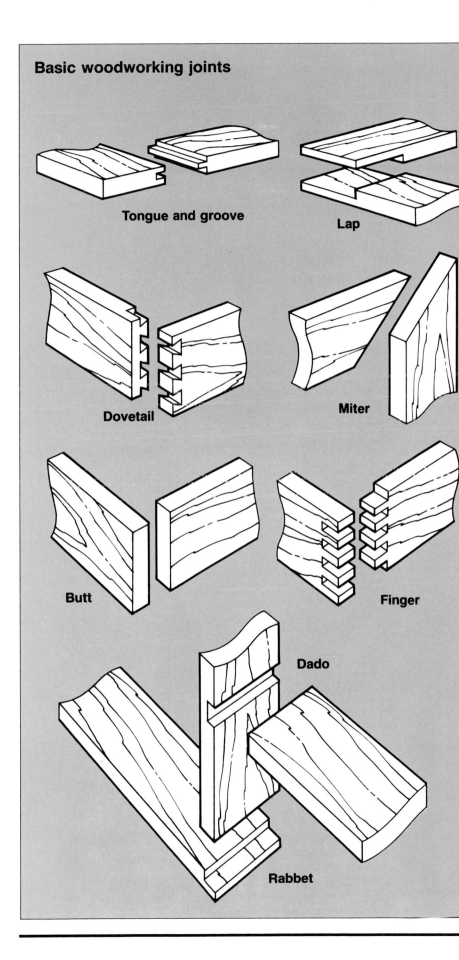

Tongue and groove

Lap

Dovetail

Miter

Butt

Finger

Dado

Rabbet

Butt:
Easy to make, but weak and unattractive; used where strength and appearance aren't primary concerns; should be strengthened with screws or nails in addition to glue.

Lap:
Used mostly to make face frames, or to join boards of the same thickness that meet at right angles.

Miter:
Used frequently as a corner joint for molding and trim; requires smooth, exact, 45-degree-angle cuts in joining pieces.

Tongue and groove:
Good for joining long boards edge-to-edge, or for making frames used in case construction.

Dovetail:
A very strong joint that also looks attractive; used in drawer and case construction; requires very exact cutting that's best done with dovetail jig, dovetail bit and router.

Finger:
Also called a box joint; a strong, attractive joint for small boxes and cases.

Dado:
Used where an edge or end of a board joins the face of a board.

Rabbet:
Used like a dado joint, but at the end of a board; also used for overlay doors and drawers.

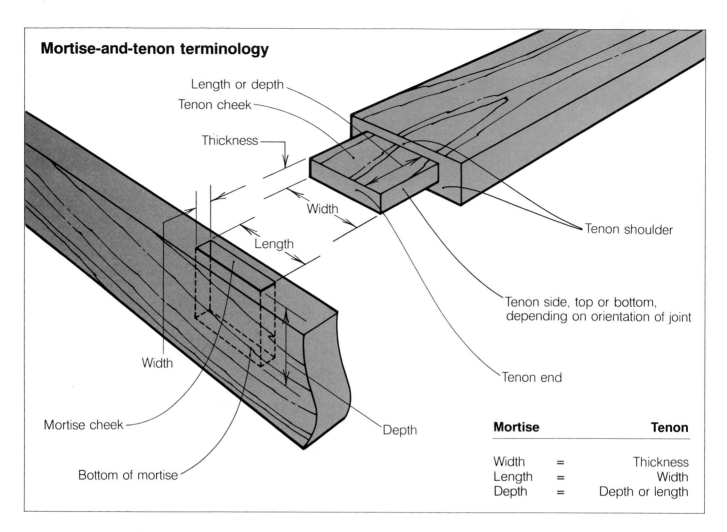

Mortise-and-tenon terminology

Length or depth
Tenon cheek
Thickness
Width
Length
Width
Mortise cheek
Bottom of mortise
Depth
Tenon shoulder
Tenon side, top or bottom, depending on orientation of joint
Tenon end

Mortise		Tenon
Width	=	Thickness
Length	=	Width
Depth	=	Depth or length

Getting serious about safety

Power tools offer significant advantages over hand tools in terms of speed and precision; but they're also more dangerous. As you use this book and whenever you're involved in a woodworking project, let safety be your first priority. Be sure to observe the following precautions.

Wear eye protection. If you wear glasses, like I do, make sure yours have shatterproof lenses. If you don't wear glasses, buy and use protective goggles that are approved for woodworking.

Check out your electrical system. Standing water, outdated or undersized wiring and ungrounded circuits are all serious hazards. If you have any doubts about the safety or capacity of your workshop's electrical system, have an electrician check it out. Good lighting is important too. I like fluorescent lights for general illumination because they're inexpensive to operate, even when they're on all day. I complement these fixed overhead lights with a couple of moveable spot lights that can be clamped in place where and when they're needed.

Use sharp tools. Whether you're trimming with a chisel or milling an edge with the router, bits and blades are a pleasure to work with when they're sharp. Dull tools add frustration to a job, and often require hazardous amounts of extra force, applied by you and (if there's a power tool involved) the motor.

Get to know your tools. To do the projects in this book safely and accurately, you'll need to have a working familiarity with a number of different power tools: how to change bits or blades; how to adjust cutting height and fence location; how much pressure to apply when feeding different stock into the set-up, and so on. Remember, it takes a while for a new tool to feel comfortable in your hands. So if you're unsure about a tool, be sure to study the owner's manual. And if a particular technique is new to you, gain some practice time on scrap stock before you start working on the good wood set aside for a specific project.

Finally, remember that safety isn't just technique and equipment; it's also an attitude. Accidents can happen more easily when you're tired, impatient or distracted. Use care and common sense when you're in the workshop and you'll be sure to get the most out of every project. Now let me show you around my workshop, and introduce some of the tools I'll be using.

Measuring and marking

The craftsman's adage "measure twice, cut once" has survived for hundreds of years, and for good reason. Successful furniture-making requires measurements that are careful and exact. I've grown accustomed to using a *tape measure* for most of my furniture-making projects. I like the rigidity of the 1-in. wide tape and the convenience of holding it in a pouch on my tool belt. A good tape will have its first few inches broken into 32nds for measurements that demand extra precision.

For squaring up and general layout work, I've got several different tools. I use my *speed square* most often because it's small and convenient to carry on my tool belt. Graduations on the body of the square enable you to measure and mark for angles other than 90 degrees. In situations where the speed square is too small for accurately squaring up work or making layout lines, I turn to my *framing square.*

The *combination square* is an adjustable square that I use for scribing a line along the edge of a board, laying out centers for holes to be drilled, or transferring measurements from one piece to another. For squaring up stock, it's not usually as accurate as the fixed squares.

Along with my speed square, my tool belt holds a sharp pencil, a *utility knife*, a *nailset* and a *12-ounce hammer* (see the color photo on page 2). These tools get used so often that they need to be close at hand. In addition to trimming joints, the utility knife keeps the pencil sharp, and can also be used to scribe razor-thin layout lines for mortising hinges and other precise work. The nailset is important because I use finishing nails on many projects. I use the nailset to drive the head of the finishing nail below the surface of the wood. This prevents hammer marks from marring the wood surface, and leaves a minute hole that can be filled with putty later.

Table saw-This is the most important power tool in my workshop. Here I'm using it to mill dadoes in the side of a desk.

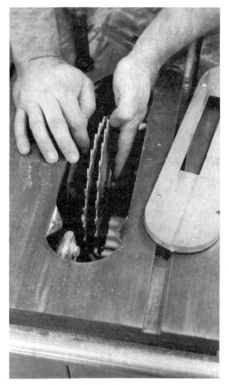

Dado head-This adjustable, twin-bladed dado head mounts on the arbor of the table saw.

The saw arsenal

The *table saw* is the most important power tool in just about any workshop. It's the workhorse you'll be using for everything from rough sizing to cutting tapered legs and milling dadoes, rabbets, tenons and even molded edges.

Because it's so important, it makes sense to invest in a good table saw. A large, heavy, stationary saw like the one I use will cost over $1,800, but there are less expensive alternatives. A 10-in. saw (one that will take a 10-in. blade) is definitely preferable to an 8-in. saw, and the motor shouldn't be rated at less than 1½ horsepower. Better saws will have large tables that are finely cast and then machined for flatness. The saw's rip fence should be easy to adjust and lock firmly in place. The miter gauge should slide smoothly in the table's slots, with little or no play to the right or left.

At a cost of around $600, a good 10-in. contractor's table saw will outlast several "handyman" models and perform more accurately. Decide which model you want, then shop around for the best price. Along with the saw, it's a good idea to buy a couple of *outfeed rollers*. These stands are designed to support large panels or boards as you cut them into smaller pieces on the table saw.

Buying a good saw blade is almost as important as buying a good saw. I use a high-quality, *carbide-tipped "combination" blade*. This type of blade can handle crosscutting (cutting across the grain of the wood) as well as ripping (cutting along the grain). Carbide teeth hold their sharpness for a long time, and a "finish-cutting" blade with 40 or 60 teeth will give you the super-smooth edge that's required for most furniture-making projects.

Panel cutter-This is a useful jig for squaring up large panels on the table saw.

With a few important accessories, your table saw's versatility increases significantly. Replacing the saw blade with a *dado head* enables you to cut a number of joints on the table saw. There are several different types of dado cutters. Mine has twin blades that tilt for different width adjustments. As with saw blades, I prefer a carbide-tipped dado cutter because it stays sharp longer than less expensive, steel-tipped cutters.

The *panel cutter* is a jig you have to make yourself. By providing a large, moving work surface (mine is made from 3/8-in. plywood), the panel cutter enables you to make straight, accurate cuts in fairly large pieces. A hardwood strip, glued and screwed to the plywood, rides in the miter gauge groove that runs parallel to the saw blade in the table top.

To mill lap joints, make raised panels, and cut long boards into shorter lengths, I use a *radial arm saw* . You can also perform these tasks on the table saw. To make smooth, exact miter joints and other angled cuts, I use a *power miter box*, which most woodworkers call a "chop box." A less expensive alternative to the chop box is a good-quality miter box designed to be used with a back saw.

For curved cuts, you'll need either a *portable jigsaw* or a *bandsaw*. I'm fortunate to have both. A good jigsaw should have variable speed control, an adjustable base and orbital cutting capability. But it still won't be able to cut thick material (especially hardwoods) with the bandsaw's speed and accuracy.

Unlike craftsmen of a century ago, I do very little sawing by hand for most of my furniture-making projects. When I do need to trim a piece of wood by hand, I use either a standard 10-point (per inch) *crosscut saw* or a fine-tooth *back saw*.

Power miter box-With a power miter box, you can make angled cuts that are precise and super-smooth.

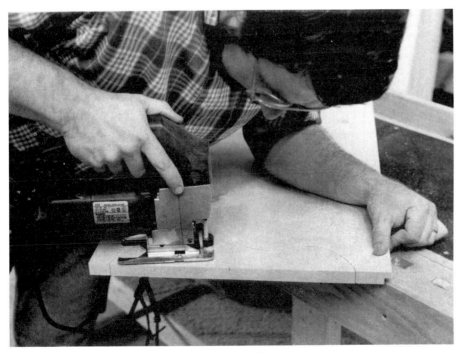

Portable jigsaw-I use the jigsaw to make curved cuts.

Bandsaw-For curves or straight cuts in extra-thick stock, the bandsaw is best.

The router table-This table is designed to hold the router upside down, with the bit pointing up. It's a useful tool for milling mortises and grooves and for molding different edges.

Router-With a router and a good selection of router bits, many different edge treatments are possible. Here I'm chamfering the top edge of the oak board that forms the back of the workbench.

Planing and shaping

Straight edges on boards are important in just about any furniture project. The typical "1x" dimension lumber that you buy from the lumber yard is fairly straight, but not as straight as it should be. In the old days, woodworkers used long, heavy "jointing planes" to shave off high spots and create flat, square edges on long boards. Today, the power-driven *jointer* does the same job, but faster and with far less effort.

Stationary jointers like the one I use are expensive but worthwhile investments if you plan to do a lot of woodworking. If you need to spend less money (or save space in your workshop), consider buying a *portable power plane*. With this lightweight power plane, you clamp your board in the workbench just as if you were going to joint an edge by hand; but instead, the power plane does the work. To work well at jointing edges, a portable power plane should have a long bed.

To mill curves and contours, I use a *router* and an assortment of bits. For making furniture, a professional-quality router is important. Many less expensive models are underpowered, and won't stand up to the heavy use that furniture building demands. The router can be used as a portable tool, or it can be mounted upside down in a *router table*. On the router table I can mill curves, grooves or mortises in smaller pieces that would be difficult to mill with the router alone.

Drilling and driving

The *portable electric drill* is the least expensive power tool in the workshop, but it plays an important role in nearly every project. For making furniture, a drill is just as important for driving screws as it is for drilling holes. The right drill to buy is a variable-speed model with a reversing switch.

I use either *brad-point drill bits* or *Forstner bits* if I'm boring holes for mortises or wood pegs. These types of bits are more expensive than conventional twist bits, but they're self-centering, and they bore clean, straight holes in any kind of wood — even through knots.

Pre-drilling screw holes and countersinking the heads is standard procedure in furniture construction. It prevents the wood from splitting, seats the screw firmly and also looks good. So I use several combination bits designed to pre-drill, countersink and counterbore screws. Sometimes called *pilot-hole bits*, these bits come in different sizes that correspond to different screw gauges.

I use *drywall screws* for general fastening, driving them with a *#2 Phillips-head bit* chucked in my drill. Despite their specialized name, drywall screws are good for all kinds of fastening jobs. They're inexpensive too, and you can buy them in just about any length. It's smart to keep a good selection on hand in the workshop.

Phillips-head bits wear out when you drive a lot of screws, so I always keep a half-dozen spares on hand, including some *#3* bits for smaller Phillips-head screws. Of course there are times when screws have to be

Driving screws-Most of the screws I use for making furniture are drywall screws, driven with a #2 Phillips-head bit chucked in the portable electric drill. Screw holes are pre-drilled and countersunk using a pilot-hole bit.

driven by hand, so I have a good selection of **straight and Phillips-head screwdrivers** too.

I've also got a **drill press** in the workshop. It's a very useful tool for drilling out mortises. Fitted with a **hollow-chisel bit**, the drill press can even mill square mortises, saving you the time of chiseling a mortise square by hand. I also use my drill press to sand curved pieces. With a drum-sanding attachment chucked in the drill, you can smooth curved edges easily and effectively.

Gluing and clamping

Glue has come a long way since the Shakers began making furniture. Like most woodworkers, I use **yellow wood glue** for all wood-to-wood joints that should be glued together. In a well-made joint, yellow glue will create a bond that's nearly impossible to break. Technically known as an "aliphatic-resin" glue, yellow woodworker's glue has only a couple of limitations. It's not waterproof, so it won't hold up in outdoor furniture, or in high humidity. The second limitation can also be an advantage: at room temperature, yellow glue sets up very quickly. Once you've applied your glue, the joint should be assembled and clamped promptly.

I apply glue straight from the bottle, then use a small brush to spread the adhesive evenly over the parts to be joined. The brush can be kept in a small can of water, along with a sponge that's good for wiping excess glue from freshly assembled joints.

Furniture joints often need some coaxing to go together tightly, and a good tool for this is a **shot-filled mallet**. Unlike the steel face of a conventional hammer, the mallet has a plastic face that won't mar the wood it strikes.

Clamps are crucial tools for furniture makers, and it's been said that you can never have too many in a workshop. There are many types of clamps. The ones you'll see me use most often are either *pipe clamps,* *C-clamps* or *spring clamps.* Pipe clamps are ideal for gluing up solid wood panels to make a table top or the side of a chest (photo 11). They're useful whenever long distances need to be spanned to clamp up large assemblies. You'll need at least 6 pipe clamps, and they should be about 4 ft. long.

C-clamps are good for many smaller jobs. I use them to hold my router table down on the workbench and to clamp small pieces together. Spring clamps can be used like C-clamps, but they can apply only limited pressure. They're good for quick, temporary assignments like holding a guide block against the table saw's rip fence during a particular milling operation.

The wood supply

Just about any wood can find some use in making furniture. Like most furniture makers, the Shakers built with native woods that they could harvest themselves or get from local sawmills. Ash, oak, cherry, maple and pine all fall into this category, and these are the species I use in this book. Depending on your taste, your budget and what you find at the lumber yard, you can use different wood than I do for any project.

If you're relatively new to furniture-making, try building with pine before you work with a hardwood like oak or cherry. Pine is every bit as traditional for furniture as the finest hardwood, and it's easier to work, whether you're using expensive power equipment or simple hand tools. Pine seasons quickly, remains relatively stable, and takes a reasonable finish.

When buying wood, I look for boards that aren't warped or twisted, and have consistent color and grain. Straight, square edges are important too, especially if you don't have a jointer. Lower grades of wood are less expensive, but more troublesome to cut and mill because of large knots, pitch pockets, warping and other imperfections.

Be sure your wood is dry. Wood that's freshly cut or wet from outdoor storage isn't good for furniture-making because it can shrink, crack and otherwise distort as it dries out. Whether I'm buying pine or an expensive wood like cherry, I ask for "kiln-dried" stock to be sure the moisture content is low.

When you're building a piece of furniture, try to avoid mixing woods in a single piece of furniture. Even though raw lumber of different species may look the same (birch and maple, for example), differences will appear as you apply finish and as the woods age.

Traditional furniture makers didn't have plywood to work with, but I'm sure they would have liked using it. Available in varying thicknesses to match different applications, plywood, masonite and particleboard offer strength, stability and flatness that's difficult to duplicate with solid wood.

In the New Yankee Workshop, I try to use these panels where they won't compromise the authenticity of the furniture: for drawer bottoms and the backs of cases and cupboards. With a face veneer of the same species as the solid wood used in a project, plywood can masquerade successfully as a solid wood panel, providing the edges remain hidden from view.

Chapter 1

Medicine cabinet

Before stamped steel medicine cabinets became standard issue in the modern house, small wooden cabinets like this one could be found in many bathrooms and dressing rooms, even in modest homes. This old-fashioned version of the medicine cabinet definitely has more warmth and craftsmanly appeal than its metal counterpart.

My medicine cabinet design is meant to be adaptable, so you shouldn't have too much trouble if you want to replace your cabinet with one you've made yourself. I built my cabinet from 3/4-in.-thick oak boards, but you could also use pine, fir or a different hardwood. Cabinet corners have box joints, a very traditional treatment for small boxes and cabinets. With a depth of $5^{1}/8$ in., my cabinet offers broader shelf space than the standard medicine cabinet. You can surface-mount this cabinet, or recess it in the wall. The door frame, with its mirror, can be hinged on either side of the cabinet.

Cutting box joints

Box joints are sometimes called "finger joints," because of the short, straight fingers that interlock in an alternating pattern. If you haven't made these joints before, you'll enjoy the challenge of building the jig described below. Once you've made the jig and mastered the technique, you can cut finger joints for many woodworking projects.

Before we get to the jig, let's cut the parts to size. The top, bottom and sides of the cabinet are all 5½ in. wide. After ripping the pieces to this width on the table saw, I cut them to their finished lengths: 24 in. for the sides and 18 in. for the top and bottom. If you're replacing a medicine cabinet that's a different size, now is the time to adjust the dimensions. The joinery details and techniques can stay the same.

I cut box joints on the table saw, using a dado head and a special jig that's screwed to the miter gauge. I adjust the dado to cut 3/8 in. wide, and raise the cutter 3/4 in. above the table. Check the miter gauge to make sure it's set for a square cut. To make the jig, you'll need a piece of 3/4-in.-thick stock about 4 in. wide and 12 in. long. Screwed on edge to the miter gauge, this piece becomes the backer board for the stock you'll be milling. You'll also need a couple of thin guide strips, or pins. In section they should measure 3/4 in. wide (the thickness of the boards you'll be milling) by 3/8 in. thick (the width of the finger joints).

To set up the jig, screw the backer board to the miter gauge and move it through the cutter to make a dado 3/8 in. wide and 3/4 in. deep. Now unscrew the backer board, move it exactly 3/8 in. to your left and screw it in place. Run the backer board through the cutter to make a second dado. Now unscrew the backer board and reattach it to the miter gauge as it was when you cut the first dado. In other words, the first dado should fit exactly over the cutter; the second dado should be located 3/8 in. to the right. Complete the jig by gluing and screwing one of the guide pins in the second dado. Leave about 2 in. of the pin protruding toward the cutter. The completed jig is shown in photo 1-1.

1-1 The jig for cutting box joints consists of a backer board that is screwed to the miter gauge and a guide pin. The 3/8-in. thickness of the guide pin matches the width of the dado cutter and the thickness of each finger in the box joint. The 3/4-in. width of the guide pin and the height of the cutter above the table should match the thickness of the stock being milled. The guide pin fits in a dado located 3/8 in. away from the cutter.

1-A Major anatomy and dimensions

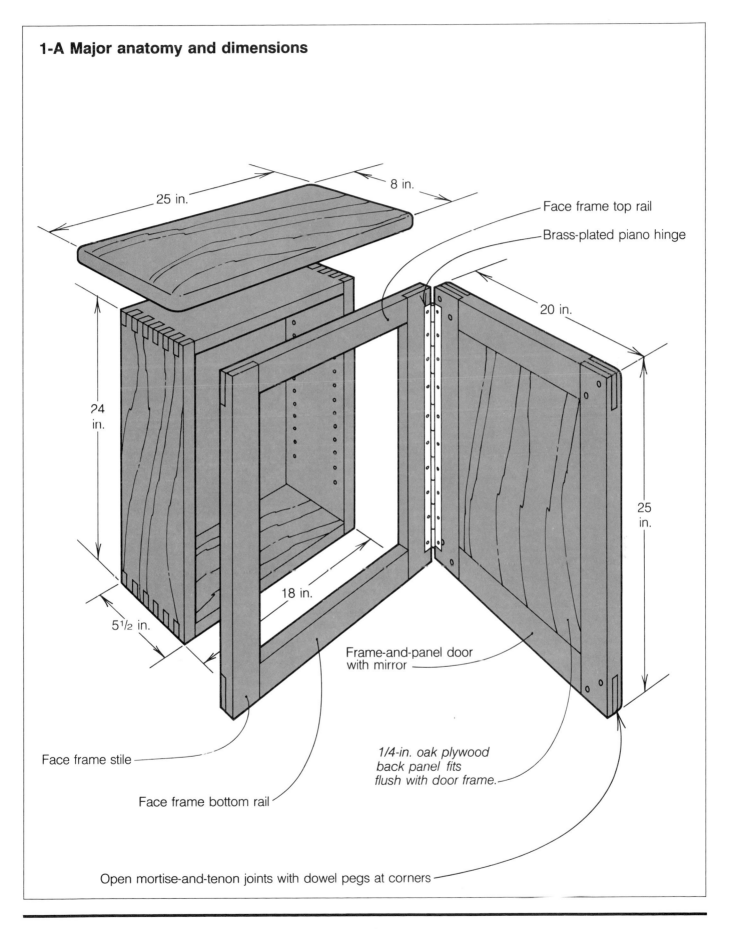

25 in.

8 in.

Face frame top rail

Brass-plated piano hinge

20 in.

24 in.

25 in.

18 in.

5¹/₂ in.

Frame-and-panel door
with mirror

Face frame stile

Face frame bottom rail

1/4-in. oak plywood
back panel fits
flush with door frame.

Open mortise-and-tenon joints with dowel pegs at corners

1-2 For the first cut, hold one side of the box vertically against the backer board. Use a loose guide pin to align the stock as shown, so that the cutter will remove a notch 3/8 in. wide and 3/4 in. high.

1-3 Place the second side of the joint in front of the first piece and position both pieces vertically against the fixed guide pin. Running the stock through the dado cutter will offset the fingers by 3/8 in.

1-4 Complete the joint by making successive cuts with both pieces held together. Place each new pair of fingers over the guide pin to align the pieces for the next cut.

For this jig to work accurately, the space between the dado and the guide pin must be exactly the same as the width of the dado cutter. The thickness of both guide pins should also match the dado's cutting width. Following the directions given below, test your jig by cutting some sample joints in scrap stock. If the cutter is too close to the fixed guide pin, your box joints will fit too loosely. Tight joints mean that the cutter is too far from the fixed pin.

To make the first cut, position the remaining guide strip vertically against the backer board and against the left edge of the pin. Now hold the cabinet side, top or bottom vertically against the backer board and guide strip and run it through the dado. This makes a notch in one corner of the stock that's 3/8 in. wide and 3/4 in. deep (see photo 1-2).

The remaining cuts to complete the joint are made with both joining pieces held in the jig. Slide the first piece against the guide pin, so that the notch you've just made fits over it. Position the second piece in front of the first piece, with one long edge butted against the guide pin. Now run both pieces through the cutter (photo 1-3). Make repeated cuts after lifting both pieces together and fitting them over the guide pin (photo 1-4).

As you complete the box joints for the rest of the cabinet, make sure to cut the top and bottom pieces so that they match; cabinet sides should likewise be identical to each other. If the sides start with a finger at each front corner, the top and bottom pieces should start with a notch.

1-5 *The jig for drilling out shelf support holes is a 1x3 clamped to a fence on the drill press. Vertical marks on the jig are spaced 1 in. apart. By aligning each end of the board with successive marks, 2 rows of identically spaced holes can be drilled.*

Drilling out for the shelves

The glass shelves for this cabinet rest on plastic supports. The supports, which you can buy in most hardware stores, are designed to fit into 1/4-in.-diameter holes drilled in the cabinet sides. Each shelf requires 4 holes, 2 in each cabinet side. Drilling a series of holes up the sides of the cabinet enables you to position the shelves according to your needs.

The 4 holes for each shelf location have to be equidistant from the bottom of the cabinet or the shelf will wobble on its supports. To make the job of drilling out the holes go quickly and accurately, I set up a special fence on the drill press. As shown in photo 1-5, the fence is a 1x3 board with vertical marks every inch. The center mark is aligned with the center of the drill chuck, and positioned 1 1/4 in. away from it. Starting 5 in. from the bottom of each side, I line up the bottom edge of the side with successive layout lines to get an exact 1-in. spacing between holes. I use a 1/4-in. brad-point bit to bore the holes, stopping the bit at 3/8-in. depth.

Box and face frame construction

Once the sides of the cabinet have been drilled out for the shelves, you can assemble the box. I use a small brush to spread glue on all the "fingers" of each joint. Then I join each corner, tapping the joint tight with a shot-filled mallet (photo 1-6).

The cabinet has a 1/4-in.-thick, oak-veneer plywood back. If the cabinet will be surface-mounted, the back should be rabbeted into the back edges of the cabinet box, as shown in drawing 1-B. I use a 3/8-in. rabbeting bit in the router for this job (photo 1-7). To recess the back slightly, I set the depth of the rabbet at 5/16 in. The bit leaves a curved edge at each corner, which I square up by hand, using a sharp chisel. As soon as this is done, I attach the back with glue and 1-in. drywall screws. When the glue in this assembly dries, I go over the sides, top and bottom of the box with a belt sander, using a medium-grit sanding belt. It's important to sand the box joints smooth and flush. Extra attention here will pay off when you apply the finish, which will highlight the joinery details.

The next step is to make up the face frame that will cover the front edges of the box. The 2 vertical frame members are called "stiles"; the horizontal members are "rails." The width of the frame is 2 in. Stiles are 25 in. long, while rails are 20 in. long. The door frame's stiles and rails are the same size as the face frame's stiles and rails, so I cut both sets of parts to size at the same time.

The face frame is joined together with lap joints. If you're looking at the cabinet from the front, the rails lap under the stiles. To mill these joints, I set up the dado head in the radial arm saw. The cutter can be adjusted for maximum width of cut, since each joint will require several passes to complete. Adjust the height of the cutter so that exactly half the thickness of the stock will be removed. If your face frame stock is 3/4 in. thick, then adjust for 3/8-in. depth of cut. Test this set-up on some scrap stock before you begin milling the lap joints.

1-6 *After spreading glue on the fingers of the joint, tap both pieces together with a shot-filled mallet.*

1-7 *With a 3/8-in. rabbeting bit in the router, I rabbet the back edge of the box to receive the plywood back. The curved corners should be chiseled square before cutting and installing the back.*

1-8 *The lap joints at the corners of the face frame are glued and screwed together. Drive a pair of #6 flat-head, 1/2-in. screws into the back of each joint to pull it tight.*

Taking care to keep the face frame square, I glue and screw the face frame together. Working from the back of the frame, I pre-drill the screw holes, using a countersink bit. Then I drive a pair of #6 flat-head, 1/2-in. screws into each joint to pull it tight (photo 1-8).

The screws in the face frame joints take the place of clamps, and allow you to attach the face frame to the box without waiting for the glue to set. As shown in drawing 1-B, the face frame is sized so that the inner edges of the bottom rail and the stiles overlap the inside of the box by 1/4 in. This creates a 1-in. overlap around the outside of the cabinet. The top of the face frame has different clearances. The top rail should fit flush with the outside of the box, which allows you to install a top shelf above the frame and door (see drawing 1-A).

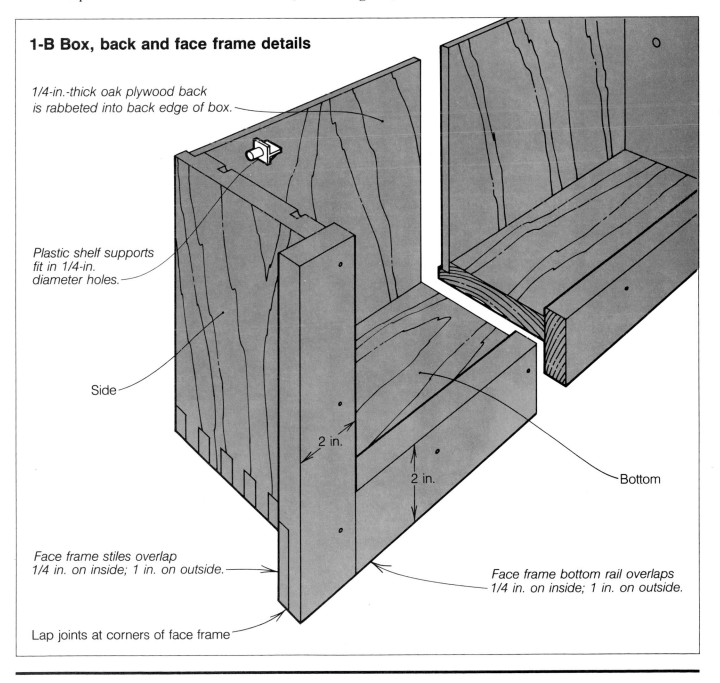

1-B Box, back and face frame details

1/4-in.-thick oak plywood back is rabbeted into back edge of box.

Plastic shelf supports fit in 1/4-in. diameter holes.

Side

2 in.

2 in.

Bottom

Face frame stiles overlap 1/4 in. on inside; 1 in. on outside.

Face frame bottom rail overlaps 1/4 in. on inside; 1 in. on outside.

Lap joints at corners of face frame

Making the mirrored door

As I mentioned earlier, the door frame is the same size as the face frame. Its joinery is a little different, though, not only for the sake of appearance, but because this frame has to hold the extra weight of a mirror. Stiles and rails join with an open mortise-and-tenon joint, also known as a bridle joint. Each corner joint is glued and pegged with a pair of 1/4-in.-thick dowels. The 1/4-in.-thick mirror rests in a groove cut all around the inside of the frame. These joinery details are shown in drawing 1-C.

I do all the door frame joinery on the table saw, starting with the open mortises. Raise the saw blade 1 1/2 in. above the table, and set the rip fence 1/4 in. away from the blade. Mill the mortises by running each stile on end through the cutter, guiding first one face, then the other, against the rip fence (photo 1-9). A third and final pass through the blade should remove the small strip of waste that remains at the center of the mortise.

The grooves for the mirror are milled next, using the dado head. Adjust it for a 1/4-in.-wide cut, and raise the cutter 1/2 in. above the table. Then set the rip fence 1/4 in. away from the cutter. This should center the groove in 3/4-in.-thick stock, but not all "1x" lumber measures exactly 3/4 in. thick. Just to make sure your set-up is right, mill a test groove in some scrap, and readjust the rip fence if necessary.

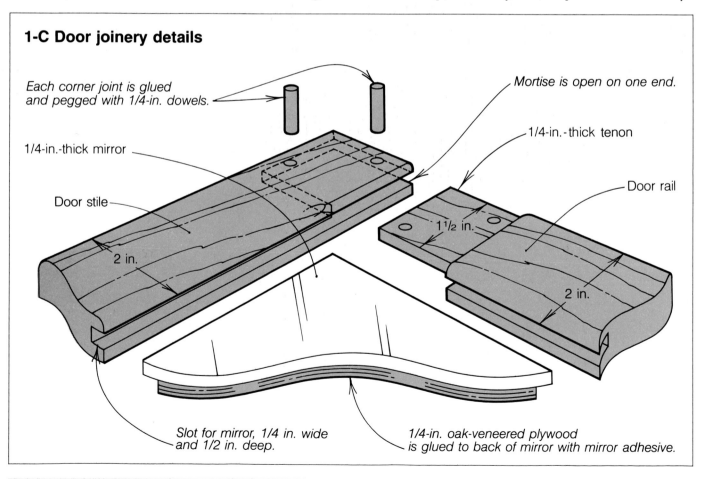

1-C Door joinery details

Each corner joint is glued and pegged with 1/4-in. dowels.

Mortise is open on one end.

1/4-in.-thick mirror

1/4-in.-thick tenon

Door stile

Door rail

2 in.

1 1/2 in.

2 in.

Slot for mirror, 1/4 in. wide and 1/2 in. deep.

1/4-in. oak-veneered plywood is glued to back of mirror with mirror adhesive.

After grooving the stiles and rails, I mill the tenons. Lower the dado cutter until it's just 1/4 in. above the table, and adjust it for maximum width of cut. The tenon shoulders and cheeks are cut with the rails held against the miter gauge. A wood gauge block, clamped to the rip fence on your side of the saw, should be positioned so that when the rail end is butted against the gauge block, the rail is aligned for its shoulder cut.

Starting on one side of the tenon, I make the shoulder cut first, then "nibble" away the rest of the waste by making several passes over the cutter. Repeat this technique for the other side of the tenon (photo 1-10). I always mill a sample tenon in some scrap stock (with the same thickness as the rails) and test its fit in the mortises I've made. This is the best way to check your set-up and be sure that your tenons will fit their mortises exactly.

When all cheek and shoulder cuts are complete, raise the cutter 1/2 in. above the table, and nibble away the inside edge of each tenon so that the tenon will clear the groove for the glass. Again, you can use the miter gauge and the wood gauge block to align the first shoulder cut on each tenon.

The next step is to dry-fit the door frame together and drill out each corner joint to receive a pair of dowel pegs. I chuck a 1/4-in. brad-point bit in the drill press, and bore 2 holes in each corner joint (photo 1-11).

1-9 Mill the mortises by running each stile on its end through the blade, guiding each face of the stock against the rip fence. To make these cuts, you'll need to brace the stock firmly, and work carefully .

1-10 To mill the tenons, I cut the shoulders first. Starting on one side, I "nibble" away the waste by making several passes over the cutter. Use the same technique on the other side of the tenon.

Hold each joint square as you bore all the way through the frame, into some scrap wood positioned beneath it.

With the frame still dry-fit together, I clamp it on the workbench between 2 bench dogs for the next operation, which is to round over the inside edge on the outside face of the frame. I use a 1/4-in. roundover bit in the router for this job. To give the bit's bearing a surface to ride on, you have to temporarily insert filler strips (1/4 in. thick and 1/2 in. wide) into the grooves inside the frame.

Now we're finally ready to put the door together. I spread glue on the mortise and tenon for each joint and then push the corner together. If necessary, use the shot-filled mallet to close the joint until the holes for the dowel pegs line up. Dab some glue on the dowels, then hammer them into their holes. The dowels should be about 1 in. long, and they should be driven in to protrude on both sides of the frame. This way, you can sand them flush after the glue dries.

Before the last frame member is glued in place, you have to slide the mirror into its slot in the frame. Check the slot for glue squeeze-out, and remove any with a dampened cloth. Then slide the mirror in place, spread glue carefully on the last pair of joints, and attach the last frame member (photo 1-12). Glue the last 4 dowel pegs in their holes.

When the glue has dried, I sand the dowels flush, using the belt sander and a fine-grit sanding belt. Even with a fine-grit belt, it only takes a moment to remove the protruding dowels, so be careful not to gouge the door frame. Finish off the outside edges of the door by going over them with a router and 3/8-in. roundover bit.

To protect the mirror and give the back of the door a more finished appearance, I glue a piece of 1/4-in.-thick plywood to the back of the mirror. Use oak-veneered plywood to match the rest of the cabinet, and cut it to fit between the stiles and rails. Before gluing the panel to the back of the mirror with mirror adhesive, give it a coat of sealer on both sides.

The cabinet door swings on a 24-in.-long piano hinge. I use a 1 1/2-in., brass-plated hinge. It can go on either side of the cabinet, so you can choose which way you want the door to open. The hinge should be mortised into the door and also into the face frame. When you lay out the location of the mortises, remember that the door should be positioned just slightly lower (1/16 in.) than the face frame it closes against. This allows the door to swing freely beneath the overhanging top shelf.

You can cut the hinge mortises by hand, but it's faster and easier to use a router. I chuck a 1/2-in. mortising bit in my router and adjust its depth of cut to match the thickness of the hinge leaf. I use a fence, attached to the router base, to mill 2 straight, even mortises 5/8 in. wide and 24 in. long. In each mortise, the 2 round corners left by the bit have to be squared up with a chisel.

Screw the hinges to the door first, then clamp the opposite leaf in its mortise on the face frame while you screw it in place. Even though the

1-11 With the door frame dry-fitted together and held square, drill out the corner joints to accept 1/4-in. dowel pegs. I use a brad-point bit to bore 2 holes in each corner.

1-12 *Slide the mirror into its slot before gluing the last frame member in place. Take care not to damage the glass when driving in the last 4 dowel pegs.*

1-13 *The door swings on a piano hinge that's mortised into the door frame and the face frame. A small Phillips-head bit, chucked in the drill, makes quick work of driving screws.*

screws for attaching the hinges are just 3/8 in. long, I pre-drill the screw holes to make them easier to drive. Driving the screws is fast and easy if you have a small Phillips-head bit to chuck in your electric drill (photo 1-13). After about half the screws are in, you can remove the clamp and finish the job.

The top shelf goes on last. With a size of 22 in. by 8¼ in., this oak shelf overhangs the front of the door by 1¼ in. and each side by 2 in. (If you decide to recess your cabinet in the wall, cut the top shelf narrower, and install it like a top trim piece after the cabinet has been screwed into its recess.) I sand the front corners of the shelf round, then round over the front and side edges with a 3/8-in. roundover bit in the router. Finally, I screw the shelf to the top of the cabinet box, counterboring 1-in. drywall screws so that I can fill the screw holes with dowel plugs.

A nice finish and a handle and catch for the door are all you need to make this cabinet ready to install. To help the medicine cabinet stand up to everyday use in moist bathroom conditions, it's important to finish the inside of the cabinet as well as the outside. I sealed the wood with a coat of sanding sealer and then applied 2 coats of satin urethane to complete the job.

Chapter 2

Workbench

The workbench is really your most important tool. Without a good one, it's difficult to work with the convenience, precision and safety that most operations require. From a more personal point of view, the workbench is a signature of sorts. Carpenters and cabinetmakers tend to compare their workbenches just as they compare completed furniture projects.

While you can buy very good woodworker's benches from different woodworking tool suppliers, it's traditional for the carpenter to make his own bench. Besides, the factory-made workbenches can cost over $500. By building your own, you'll save enough money to buy a new router, or the wood for several furniture projects.

My workbench is a lightweight version of the traditional European-style benches that most cabinetmakers use. Like the classic cabinetmaker's bench, this one is designed to use bench dogs and a heavy-duty bench vice. An integral tool tray runs the full length of the bench along its back side, and there's a lower shelf for storing lumber or tools. Instead of using hardwood for the entire bench, my version has a frame that's made from common 2x4s. The workbench top is 1/4-in.-thick tempered masonite, screwed to a 3/4-in.-thick plywood base. The masonite may not look as impressive as a top of laminated oak or maple, but it's inexpensive and easy to replace when it gets overloaded with scratches and stains.

There is some oak in my workbench, but it's used selectively. For example, the oak edge boards look good and provide longer wear at the bench perimeter than softwood could offer. It's also important for the tailstock assembly and bench dogs to be made from oak. These are the moving parts of the bench, and they need hardwood's extra density, strength and durability.

2x4 frame
The entire frame for the workbench is made from 2x4s. Though there

are quite a few parts, the joinery details are fairly simple. Frame members join with either lap joints, rabbets or dadoes. As shown in drawing 2-A, joint width is either 1¹/₂ in. (the thickness of a standard 2x4), 3 in. (a pair of 2x4s joined face-to-face) or 3¹/₂ in. (standard 2x4 width). Joint depth is a uniform 1/2 in.

The first step in building the frame is to cut all frame members to their finished lengths. Once this is done, you can begin marking up the stock with layout lines for all the joints (refer to drawing 2-A). To avoid mistakes, it's smart to make easily visible "X" marks in the "waste" areas that will be removed. This is a good way to avoid cutting a joint on the wrong side of the stock. It's also a good idea to label the frame members so that you'll have no problems identifying them later.

It's best to mill all frame joints in one session at the radial arm saw (photo 2-1). Install the dado cutter and adjust it for maximum width of cut. Then adjust the height of the saw so that the dado will cut 1/2 in. deep in a 2x4 laid flat on the radial arm's table. Make some test cuts in scrap 2x4s to make sure the depth of cut is exactly 1/2 in. When the depth adjustment is right, you're ready to cut the joints. Take your time, moving the cutter through the stock with firm, even pressure.

The bench stop assembly is part of the frame too. Unlike the other frame members, its dadoes aren't cut at a right angle. For this reason, don't cut the bench stop dadoes until all the right-angled joints have been made in the other frame members.

As shown in drawing 2-B, the bench stop assembly is made by joining identical 2x4 halves together. Each half starts out as a 46-in.-long 2x4. A series of 8 dadoes are milled in each piece, 6 in. apart. Dado depth is 3/8 in. Width is 1 in. and the angle of the dado is 4 degrees off square, or 86 degrees. This angle is important. For the bench dogs to work

2-1 Lap and dado joints for the 2x4 frame are cut in one long session at the radial arm saw. Depth of cut stays at 1/2 in., while each joint requires several passes with the dado cutter set at maximum width.

2-A Joint layout for 2x4 frame

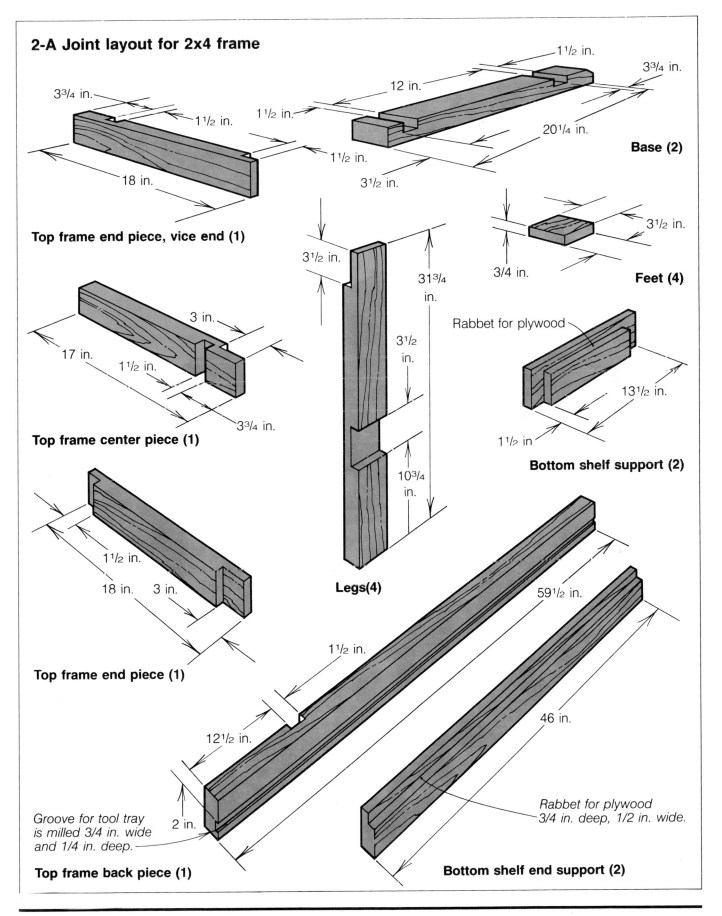

3³/₄ in.
1¹/₂ in.
18 in.

Top frame end piece, vice end (1)

1¹/₂ in.
12 in.
1¹/₂ in.
3³/₄ in.
20¹/₄ in.
3¹/₂ in.
1¹/₂ in.

Base (2)

3 in.
17 in.
1¹/₂ in.
3³/₄ in.

Top frame center piece (1)

3¹/₂ in.
3/4 in.
3¹/₂ in.

Feet (4)

3¹/₂ in.
31³/₄ in.
3¹/₂ in.
10³/₄ in.

Legs(4)

Rabbet for plywood
13¹/₂ in.
1¹/₂ in.

Bottom shelf support (2)

1¹/₂ in.
18 in.
3 in.

Top frame end piece (1)

59¹/₂ in.
1¹/₂ in.
46 in.

Rabbet for plywood
3/4 in. deep, 1/2 in. wide.

Bottom shelf end support (2)

Groove for tool tray
is milled 3/4 in. wide
and 1/4 in. deep.
12¹/₂ in.
2 in.

Top frame back piece (1)

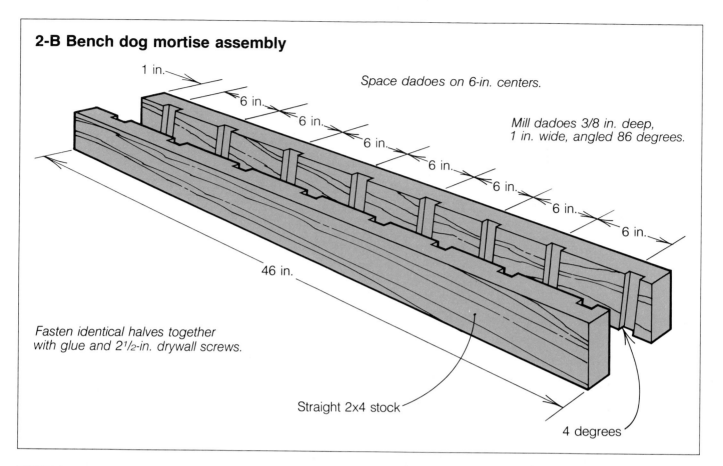

2-B Bench dog mortise assembly

1 in.

6 in.

6 in.

6 in.

6 in.

6 in.

6 in.

6 in.

Space dadoes on 6-in. centers.

Mill dadoes 3/8 in. deep, 1 in. wide, angled 86 degrees.

46 in.

Fasten identical halves together with glue and 2½-in. drywall screws.

Straight 2x4 stock

4 degrees

2-2 Dadoes for the bench dog assembly are milled 1 in. wide and 3/8 in. deep, with the radial arm saw adjusted to cut at an 86-degree angle.

2-3 Use an alignment block when fastening the matching halves of the bench dog assembly together. The block is also helpful for removing glue squeeze-out inside the mortises.

2-C Top frame construction

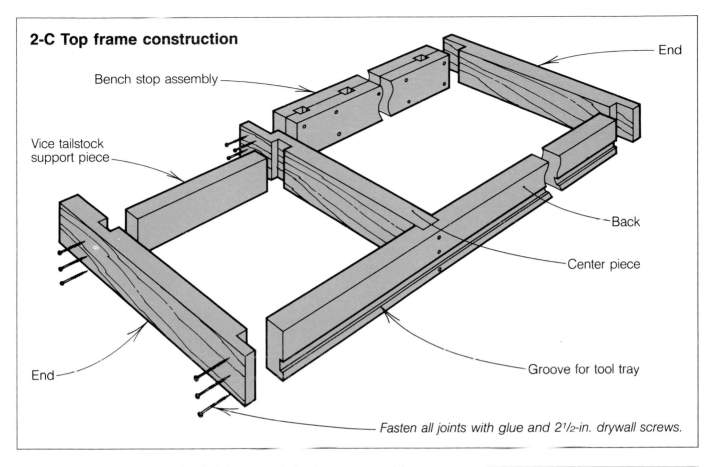

Bench stop assembly

End

Vice tailstock support piece

Back

Center piece

End

Groove for tool tray

Fasten all joints with glue and 2¹/₂-in. drywall screws.

correctly, they need to slant slightly toward the bench vice. After adjusting the radial arm saw to make the 86-degree cut, mill the dadoes in both 2x4s (photo 2-2).

The next step is to glue and screw the 2x4s together, transforming the dadoed halves into a single piece with 8 slanted mortises. I spread glue on the inside faces of the 2x4s, taking care not to leave excess glue in the dadoes. Then I use a piece of wood to align the 2x4s while I pre-drill the screw holes and drive 2¹/₂-in. drywall screws to pull the pieces together (photo 2-3). In section, your alignment piece should be a close match for the dimensions of the mortises: 3/4 in. thick by 1 in. wide. Take care to drive your screws between the mortises, and work the alignment piece back and forth in each mortise to smooth out any globs of glue.

With the bench stop assembly complete, you're ready to put the workbench frame together. Start with the top first. In addition to the bench stop assembly, there are two end pieces, a long back piece, a center piece, and a short 2x4 piece that holds part of the vice tailstock assembly (see drawing 2-C). Be sure that the bench stop assembly is oriented with its mortises facing toward the vice end of the bench. Using glue and 2¹/₂-in. drywall screws, I fasten all these parts together (photo 2-4).

The legs come next. Flip the top upside down. The lap joint at the top of each leg fits against the inside of the top's frame. Install the legs

2-4 The top frame includes the bench dog assembly. I use glue and 2¹/₂-in. drywall screws to join all the parts together.

at the corners of the rectangle created by the center piece, the bench top assembly, the end piece, and the long back piece. I glue and screw the legs in place, using a framing square to keep the legs square with the top when installing them (photo 2-5).

When the legs are on, you can attach the bottom shelf supports. The long supports fit into 3 1/2-in.-wide dadoes cut in the legs. The short supports are rabbeted to overlap the ends of the long supports. All 4 pieces are rabbeted along their inside top edges to hold the plywood shelf.

Attach the base and feet next. The bottom ends of the legs should fit into dadoes in the 2 base pieces. When you've screwed the base pieces to the legs, attach the feet. These 3/4-in.-thick pads go at the outer edges of the base pieces, and give the bench additional stability on rough or uneven floors (photo 2-6). As soon as the feet are on, flip the bench right side up and drop in the plywood shelf (photo 2-7).

A 2-layer top

On this bench, the 3/4-in.-thick plywood top is permanent. The 1/4-in.-thick masonite work surface that covers it is replaceable. But both sheets are the same size and require the same cut-outs. So after cutting the sheets individually to their finished length (61 1/2 in.) and width (18 in.), I screw them together with a couple of 1/2-in.-long screws. This saves some time in cutting both sheets for the bench dog slot and vice tailstock.

The bench dog slot is 43 1/4 in. long. The slot starts 1 3/4 in. from the vice end of the top, and extends to within 3 in. of the opposite end.

2-5 I hold each leg against the framing square while screwing it to the top frame of the bench.

2-6 Keeping the frame upended, attach the dadoed base pieces to the legs; then screw the feet to the base.

2-7 With the frame right side up, slide the lower plywood shelf into its rabbeted frame and screw it down.

To cut out the slot, I carefully lower the sheets over the table saw blade, guiding the stock against the rip fence as shown in photo 2-8. I run the plywood flat against the table until the blade nears the end of the slot; then I lift the sheet free. To square the ends, I use a portable jigsaw.

Now screw both plywood and masonite to the top frame of the bench. I drive $1^5/8$-in. drywall screws through both layers into frame members. To avoid distorting or dimpling the masonite, it's a good idea to pre-drill holes using a countersink bit. With the top secured, you can make the cut-out for the vice. The cut follows the rectangular opening described by the 2x4 frame near the front corner of the bench. Using a square, transfer the layout lines to the masonite, and cut out as much as you can with a circular saw (photo 2-9). You'll have to finish the cut-out with either a a crosscut saw or a portable jigsaw.

The tailstock

The tailstock has a pair of bench dog mortises, and is designed to slide back and forth on runners, driven by the vice screw mechanism (see drawing 2-D). The entire assembly, including sides, runners, end piece and the tailstock itself, should be made from hardwood. I chose oak

2-8 Keep the 2-layer top of the workbench together when cutting out the 3/4-in.-wide bench dog slot. Using the rip fence as a guide, the top has to be lowered down over the blade to make the cut, then raised free when the blade reaches the end of the slot. After making a pair of parallel cuts, square up the slot ends with a portable jigsaw.

2-9 Cut out the tailstock opening after screwing the top to the frame. To cut the long side of the opening, you'll have to make a pocket cut, carefully lowering the blade down into the top. Finish cutting out the corners of the opening with a hand saw.

stock, but maple, birch or even cherry will do just as well. All the parts for the tailstock assembly can be made from 3/4-in.-thick stock, except for the tailstock itself. For this, you'll need two pieces that are 1⁷/₁₆ in. thick, 4¹/₂ in. wide and 6 in. long. If you don't have solid oak in this thickness, you can glue together 3/4-in.-thick stock and then plane or sand it down to the right thickness.

I cut all the dadoes for the tailstock assembly on the table saw, with the dado head adjusted for 3/4-in. width and 3/8-in. depth. You'll have to cut 4 dadoes for the runners that the tailstock slides on. Do this with the rip fence set up 1⁷/₈ in. away from the cutter. Run both tailstock halves through the cutter, using the rip fence as a guide; then run the inner runner block through. The bench front piece needn't be dadoed along its entire length. Instead, you can lift the stock free of the cutter after cutting a 12-in.-long dado. Screw the oak runners to the inner runner block and front piece with 3/4-in. drywall screws, driven through

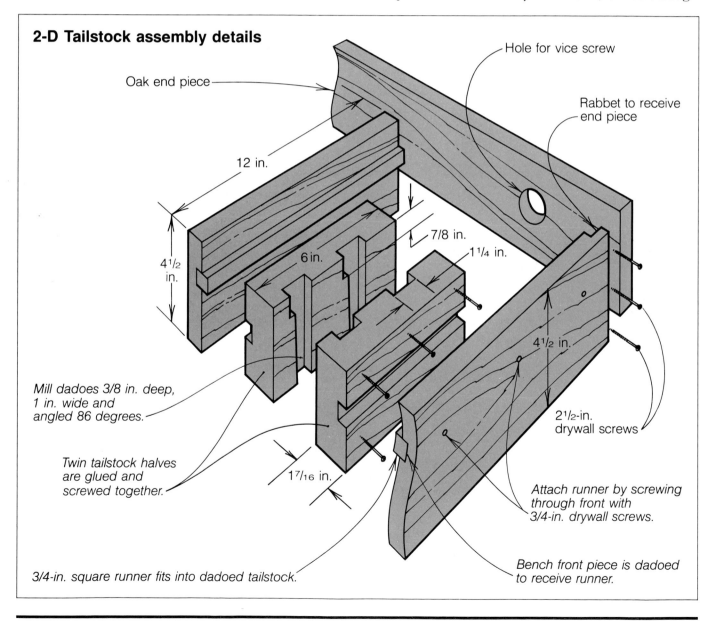

2-D Tailstock assembly details

Hole for vice screw

Oak end piece

Rabbet to receive end piece

12 in.

7/8 in.

6 in.

1¹/₄ in.

4¹/₂ in.

4¹/₂ in.

Mill dadoes 3/8 in. deep, 1 in. wide and angled 86 degrees.

2¹/₂-in. drywall screws

Twin tailstock halves are glued and screwed together.

1⁷/₁₆ in.

Attach runner by screwing through front with 3/4-in. drywall screws.

3/4-in. square runner fits into dadoed tailstock.

Bench front piece is dadoed to receive runner.

the back of the dado, as shown in drawing 2-D.

The 2 dadoes for the the bench dogs are 3/8 in. deep and 1 in. wide. These dadoes have to be cut so that they lean 4 degrees toward the mortises in the bench dog assembly. I adjust the miter gauge to 86 degrees and use it to guide the stock through the cutter. Because the stock is short, I clamp a wood auxiliary fence to the gauge to give me a better grip on the work (photo 2-10). It takes a couple of passes to cut each 1-in.-wide dado. After the tailstock's dadoes are cut, glue and screw both halves together. Pre-drill the screw holes and drive 2¹/₂-in. drywall screws from both sides of the assembly. Use a scrap piece of wood to scrape the insides of the mortises and remove glue squeeze-out.

The next step is to enlarge the top of each tailstock mortise so that the bench dogs can be pushed down flush with the bench surface. The tops of the 2 mortises have to be drilled out (to a depth of 7/8 in.) and chiseled square to match the 1¹/₄-in. by 3/4-in. size of each bench dog at its upper end. I use a 3/8-in. Forstner bit in the drill press to drill out the mortises. You could also do this work with a portable electric drill. Finish by squaring up the tops of both mortises with a sharp 1/2-in. chisel.

Before you install the tailstock, it's important to go over all the parts with some medium-grit sandpaper. You don't want to leave any sharp edges, dried glue or other irregularities that might impair the movement of the vice. Check the tailstock for a smooth fit in its runners. When you're satisfied, start the installation by screwing the inner vice runner block in place. Its top edge should be flush with the masonite top. Install the 2 oak end pieces next by driving 1⁵/₈-in. drywall screws into the top frame. Take care to countersink all screws. The long oak front piece and the tailstock are the last pieces to go on, and they have to be installed together.

The end piece and 2x4 frame member on the vice end of the bench will both have to be drilled out for the bench screw. The installation

2-11 To install the bench screw, you have to drill through the end of the bench and screw mounting plates to the tailstock and to the oak end piece. The wood handle is made by fastening round door pulls to a 12-in. length of 1-in.-diameter dowel rod.

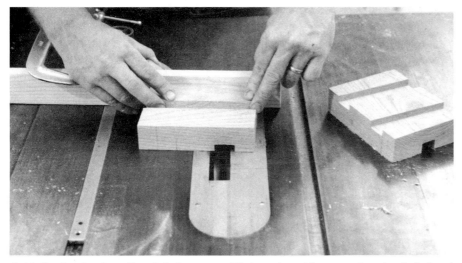

2-10 Dadoes in the tailstock halves are milled on the table saw, using the dado head. A wood auxiliary fence, clamped to the miter gauge, helps to hold the stock.

instructions for my bench screw call for a 1½-in.-diameter hole. After the hole is drilled, you have to remove the oak front piece and the tailstock to install the threaded sleeve and the end nut that complete the bench screw assembly (see photo 2-11). Once these parts have been fastened to the frame and the tailstock, the oak front piece and tailstock can be screwed back in place.

My bench screw didn't come with a handle, so I had to make one. This turned out to be easier than I expected. Instead of turning a handle on the lathe, I cut a 10-in. length of 1-in.-thick dowel and attached round wood drawer knobs to both ends of the dowel after sliding it through the vice screw handle. I used glue and 3/8-in. dowels to join the drawer knobs to the dowel rod.

To the dogs

The smallest parts get made last. The bench dogs and their backer blocks are cut from 3/4-in.-thick oak stock. I make a pair of bench dogs first, then use them as guides when cutting and installing the backer blocks. The dogs are designed so that they can easily be pushed down flush with the bench top when not in use. Screwed to the dog body, a thin oak spring strip holds the dog in place above the table surface while you're using the vice (see drawing 2-E).

To make each dog, I start with a small rectangle of oak at least 6 in. long and 1¼ in. wide. After laying out the angled form of the dog on the stock, I cut it out on the bandsaw (photo 2-12). Then I attach the 5-in.-long spring strips with 1/2-in. screws, driven into the slanted lower portion of the dog. Be sure to pre-drill the screw holes and countersink the heads. It's easy to split the 1/8-in.-thick strips when attaching them, so drive the screws carefully (photo 2-13).

The bench dog backer blocks are 1 in. wide and just shy (about 1/16 in.) of 4¾ in. long, the distance between mortises. Like the mortises

2-12 After tracing layout lines onto a small piece of 3/4-in.-thick oak. I cut out the body of the bench dog on the bandsaw.

2-13 Fasten oak spring strips to the bench dogs with 1/2-in. flat-head screws. To avoid splitting the strips, pre-drill the screw holes, countersink the heads and drive the screws carefully.

2-14 Use a pair of 1⅝-in. drywall screws to fasten each bench dog backer block to the bench dog assembly. Bench dogs, positioned in adjacent mortises, can be used to check the fit and alignment of backer blocks before you screw them down.

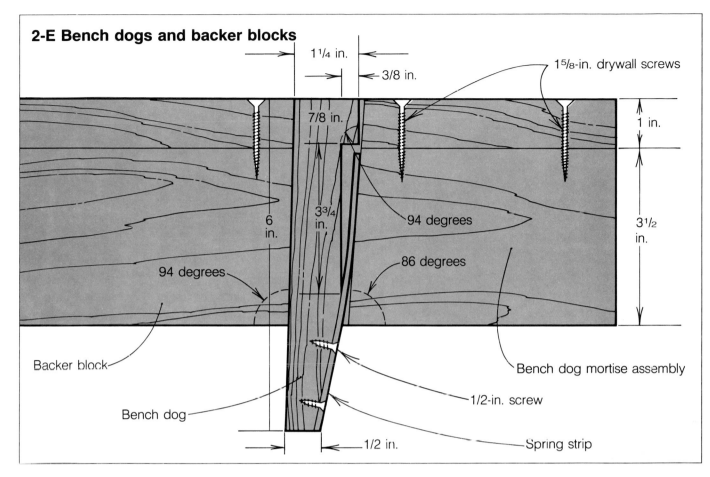

2-E Bench dogs and backer blocks

1¼ in.

3/8 in.

1⅝-in. drywall screws

7/8 in.

1 in.

6 in.

3¾ in.

94 degrees

3½ in.

94 degrees

86 degrees

Backer block

Bench dog mortise assembly

1/2-in. screw

Bench dog

Spring strip

1/2 in.

and the dogs, the backer blocks need to be cut 4 degrees off square. For the bench dogs to operate smoothly, each backer block needs to be just the right length. I test the length of each block by fitting it in its position between mortises and then inserting the 2 bench dogs. It's best to start with a block that's too long and trim it back until the dogs fit just right. One by one, I anchor each block to the bench with glue and a pair of 1⅝-in. drywall screws (photo 2-14).

Finishing up

The tool tray at the back of the bench is all that's left to make. I screw a 2-in.-wide oak trim strip to the top frame along the front edge of the tool tray. The tray itself is made by sliding a 3/4-in.-thick plywood bottom piece into 1/4-in.-deep dadoes cut in both oak end pieces and in the back frame member. Attach the back of the tray last. This 4½-in.-wide oak piece is also dadoed to fit over the bottom, and rabbeted at both ends to fit over the oak side pieces.

Drive some extra 1⅝-in. drywall screws through the oak edge pieces and into the top frame of the bench, and also screw together the rabbeted joints at the corners of the bench. As a finishing touch, I go over the oak edges with a chamfering bit chucked in the router (photo 2-15). Chamfered corners look nicer than sharp, square ones; and they're less likely to splinter as you put the bench to use.

2-15 With a router and chamfering bit, I chamfer the oak edges all around the bench.

Chapter 3

Drop-leaf table

The drop-leaf table is one of those furniture pieces that never lose their appeal. Its simple, durable design makes it as elegant as it is useful. Fully open, this table can take on half a dozen diners. But as soon as the plates are cleared, you can drop the leaves and let the table assume its less substantial identity. Countless versions of the drop-leaf table exist, with slight changes in proportions and detailing. You'll also find these tables made from many different kinds of wood, including pine, cherry, oak, walnut and even mahogany or teak. I chose white ash, a wood that I don't get a chance to work with very often. Though light-colored, ash can have a wild grain, especially in flat-sawn boards. Ash is nearly as hard as oak, but not quite as dense. Strong, resilient and still relatively light, it's the traditional wood for baseball bats. If you've got any stock left over after building this table, you might try turning your own "Louisville Slugger."

Turning the legs

The legs for this table start out as "blanks" that are 2 in. square and 32 in. long. I choose leg blanks that are straight and clear, because you don't want knots or imperfections in wood that's to be turned. The top $6^7/8$ in. of each leg remains square, but the rest of the leg is turned, following a pattern that I took from an antique table (see drawing 3-B). I find the turning centers on each blank by crossing diagonals at both ends.

Because the profile of the turned legs is fairly intricate, I decided to set up a duplicating jig on the lathe to make it easier to produce 4 identical turnings. The jig that I use is a factory-made one designed for my lathe. It works a lot like the key-duplicating machines you'll find at most hardware stores. The first thing I do is to bandsaw a full-scale

3-1 Cut from masonite and mounted directly above the leg blank on the lathe, the leg pattern serves as a guide in this duplicating jig. As an indexing pin moves toward the pattern, the cutter directly below it removes wood from the blank.

template, or pattern, of the leg profile in 1/4-in.-thick masonite. The jig will also handle a leg that's already turned instead of a pattern, but I didn't have an existing leg to use. After clamping the pattern in the jig, I align the jig directly over the lathe's turning centers.

Next, I set up the cutting and indexing assembly, which rests on a small table and is designed to make the cutter conform to the contours of the pattern. As an indexing pin moves toward the pattern, the cutter moves into the stock, removing the waste that stands in the way of the finished turning. When the indexing pin contacts the pattern, the cutter has reached its full depth of cut. When I mount the leg blank in the lathe, I make sure that there's room at both ends of the blank for trimming the leg to its final length of 27 3/8 in. With the blank in place, the cutting and indexing assembly gives me a rough idea of how much stock needs to be removed from the blank. To make the turning work go a little easier, I remove the blank and trim it on all 4 corners, using the bandsaw. Then I re-mount the blank in the lathe and begin turning.

It takes a while to get a feel for using this jig. A firm grip on the cutting and indexing assembly is important, and you have to work up and down the pattern, removing wood gradually. I use a slow speed on the lathe when roughing out the leg. At this stage, you're just rounding off the stock, and the indexing pin isn't close enough to the pattern to actually contact it. When the pin gets closer to the pattern, I switch to a higher speed for shaping. Now you'll see the turning profile start to emerge (photo 3-1).

3-A Major anatomy and dimensions

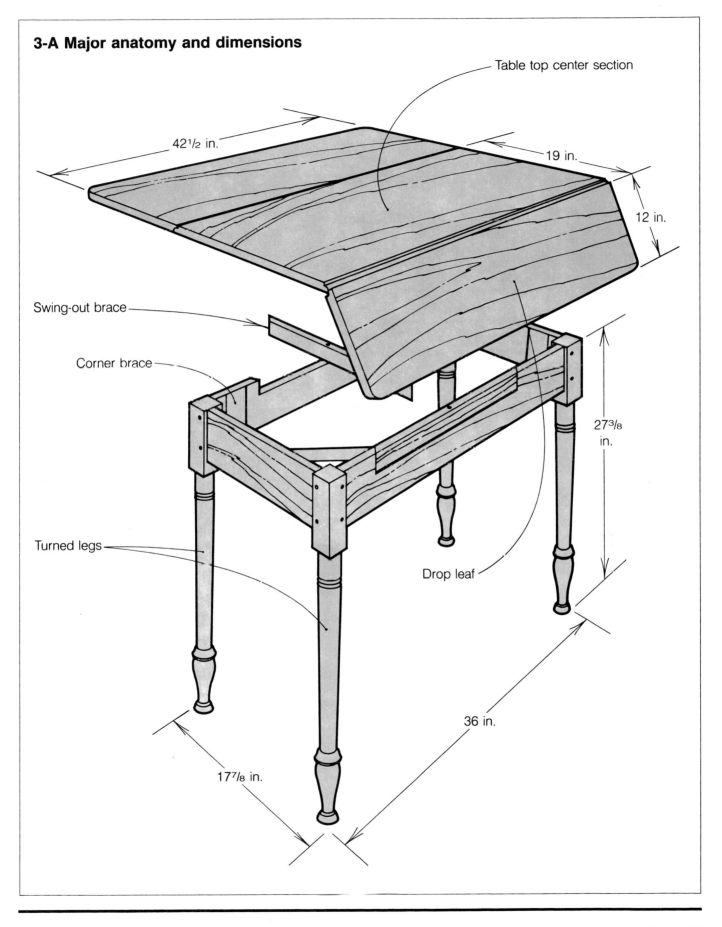

Table top center section

42¹/₂ in.

19 in.

12 in.

Swing-out brace

Corner brace

27³/₈ in.

Turned legs

Drop leaf

17⁷/₈ in.

36 in.

3-B Turned leg profile

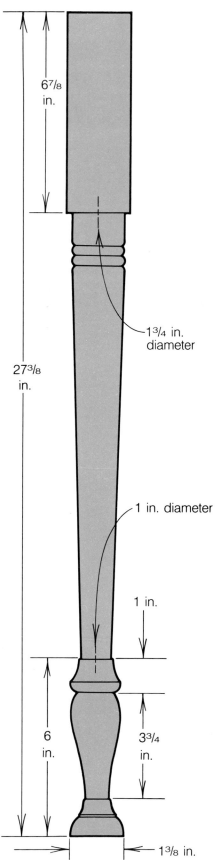

6⁷/₈ in.

1³/₄ in. diameter

27³/₈ in.

1 in. diameter

1 in.

6 in.

3³/₄ in.

1³/₈ in.

When you've cut and smoothed the leg as far as the jig will allow, switch to a higher speed and smooth the turned surfaces with some medium-grit sandpaper. Finally, switch to fine grit and keep going over the wood until it's smooth enough to receive a coat of finish. Repeat these steps for each leg. Wait till all 4 legs are turned and sanded before you cut them to their finished length.

Mortises and tenons

The next step is to mortise the legs so that they can be joined to the rails, completing the base of the table. Each leg needs 2 mortises. They're 3/8 in. wide, 4 in. long, and 3/4 in. deep. The mortises start 1/2 in. down from the top of the leg. I layout each mortise 5/16 in. away from the outside face of the leg. This creates a 1/8-in. reveal, or offset, where the rails meet the legs (see drawing 3-C).

I mill the mortises on the drill press, using a 3/8-in.-wide hollow-chisel mortiser. I set up a fence on the drill press table to keep the mortise 5/16 in. away from the face of the leg, and adjust the boring depth to 3/4 in. When using the mortising bit, the first cut is the hardest because there's wood on all 4 sides of the bit. I drill out the top and bottom of the mortise first, then remove the waste from the center (photo 3-2).

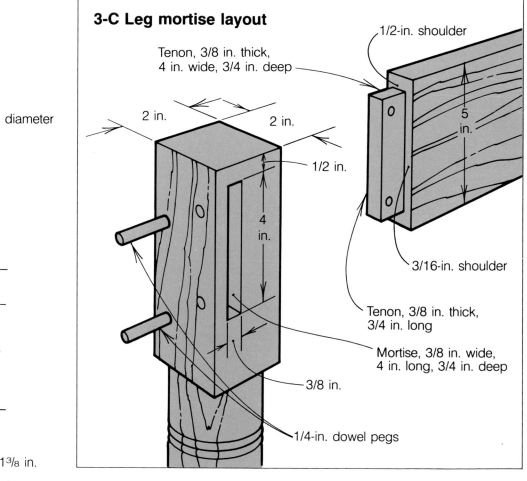

3-C Leg mortise layout

Tenon, 3/8 in. thick, 4 in. wide, 3/4 in. deep

1/2-in. shoulder

2 in.

2 in.

5 in.

1/2 in.

4 in.

3/16-in. shoulder

Tenon, 3/8 in. thick, 3/4 in. long

Mortise, 3/8 in. wide, 4 in. long, 3/4 in. deep

3/8 in.

1/4-in. dowel pegs

The rails are 5 in. wide and 3/4 in. thick. Side rails measure 33½ in. long, including tenons. End rails are 15½ in. long. After cutting the stock to these dimensions, I mill the tenons on the table saw. Matching the mortises in the legs, the tenons are 3/8 in. thick, 4 in. wide and 3/4 in. long (see drawing 3-C). You'll be setting up the saw several different ways to make the tenons, and each set-up should be tested on some scrap stock before you run your rails through it. Running a test cut enables you to correct any slight inaccuracies in blade height or fence location without ruining your good stock.

Cut the tenon shoulders first. Raise the blade 3/16 in. above the table, set your miter gauge for a 90-degree cut, and clamp a wood gauge block to the rip fence on your side of the saw. Now adjust the rip fence so that the gauge block is 3/4 in. away from the outside edge of the blade's cutting line. In other words, when the end of the rail is butted against the gauge block, the rail will be lined up for its shoulder cut. This set-up is shown in photo 3-3. Each tenon requires 2 shoulder cuts.

Next, trim 1/2 in. from the top and bottom of each tenon. To do this, keep the gauge block where it is, raise blade height to 1/2 in., and run the rails on edge through the set-up (photo 3-4). I make the shoulder cut first, then "nibble" away the rest of the waste by making repeated passes through the blade.

The tenon cheeks are cut last. Remove the gauge block, set the rip fence 9/16 in. away from the blade and adjust blade height to 3/4 in. Run the rails vertically through this set-up, as shown in photo 3-5. A pair of cheek cuts completes each tenon.

3-2 A hollow-chisel mortising bit makes quick work of milling mortises in the legs. A fence keeps the leg aligned while repeated plunge-cuts are made with the bit.

3-3 The shoulders of the rail tenons are cut first. To align the rail end for the shoulder cut, use the miter gauge and a wood gauge block that's clamped to the rip fence. Blade height should be 3/16 in. for a 3/8-in.-wide tenon.

3-4 With the gauge block in the same position, cut the shoulders on the top and bottom of each tenon. Blade height should be 1/2 in. Make repeated passes with the stock held on edge against the miter gauge to finish each shoulder.

3-5 To cut the tenon cheeks, position the rip fence 9/16 in. away from the blade and raise the blade 3/4 in. above the table. Run the tenons on end through the blade, using the rip fence as a guide. Each tenon needs 2 cheek cuts.

Swing-out braces

The table's swing-out braces are cut right out of the side rails. Brace width is 1⅝ in., and length is 21 in. Because the ends of the braces are cut on a 45-degree angle, each brace can swing only one way (see drawing 3-D). For the braces to be parallel when they open, they can't be centered along the top of the rail. Instead, the pivot point for each brace is offset 1 in. from the center of its rail.

Details for laying out the braces are shown in drawing 3-E. The first step is to mark the pivot points. When this is done, measure 10½ in. on either side of the point to find the full length of the brace. Note the configuration of the 45-degree angles, and remember that the full length is from one tip of the brace to the other. You need to pre-drill the screw holes, and the best time to do this is before cutting out the braces. I use my portable drill, setting my speed square next to the rail to help me keep the drill bit plumb (photo 3-6).

It's a little tricky to cut the braces from the rails. To cut out most of the length of the brace, I use a thin-kerf blade in the table saw. After setting the rip fence 1¾ in. away from the blade, I carefully lower the rail over the blade and cut as far along the layout line as I can (photo 3-7). It's all right for the saw kerf to extend slightly beyond the end of the brace, as long as this kerf is on the inside of the rail, where it won't be seen. Cut the angled ends of the braces with a back saw (photo 3-8). Once these pieces are free, go over the sawn surfaces and smooth any irregularities with some medium-grit sandpaper.

As soon as the braces are out, they can be fastened back in place, with screws and washers. The washers, positioned between the brace

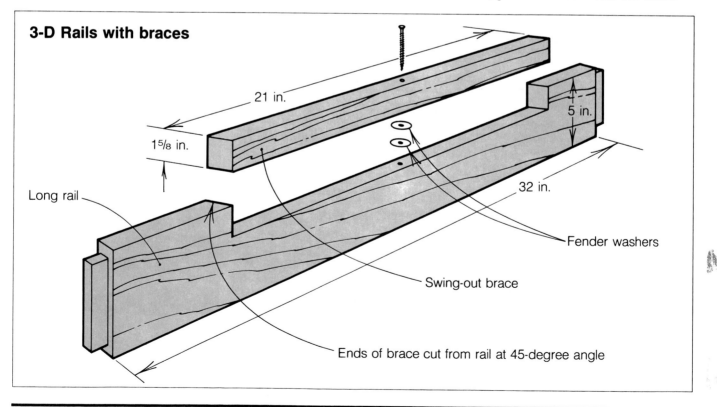

3-D Rails with braces

21 in.

1⅝ in.

5 in.

32 in.

Long rail

Fender washers

Swing-out brace

Ends of brace cut from rail at 45-degree angle

3-E Brace layout

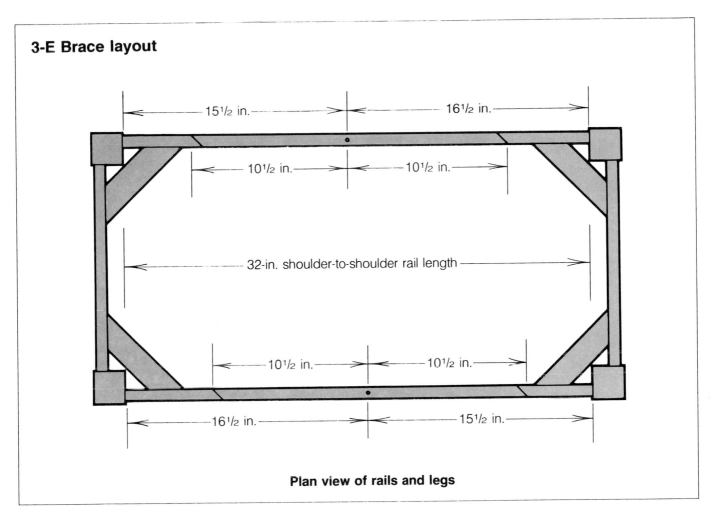

← 15½ in. → ← 16½ in. →

← 10½ in. → ← 10½ in. →

← 32-in. shoulder-to-shoulder rail length →

← 10½ in. → ← 10½ in. →

← 16½ in. → ← 15½ in. →

Plan view of rails and legs

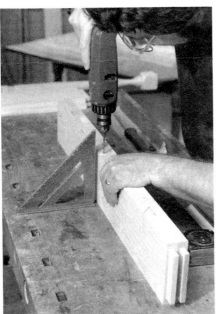

3-6 After laying out the braces, pre-drill the screw hole at each brace pivot point. A speed square serves as a guide for keeping the bit plumb.

3-7 Carefully lower the rail down over the blade to cut out the bottom edge of the brace. Set the rip fence 1¾ in. away from the blade.

3-8 With the rail clamped in the workbench, I use a back saw to cut out the end of the brace at a 45-degree angle. A second end-cut frees the brace.

3-9 *With a coat of glue applied, the rail tenon gets fitted into its mortise.*

and the rail, let this pivot point function more smoothly. They also make up for the wood lost to the saw kerf, bringing the top edge of the brace flush with the top edge of the rail. On my table, a pair of "fender" washers raises each brace just the right height. I drive a 2½-in. drywall screw through the brace and washers and into the rail. The screw head has to be countersunk, and the screw shouldn't be driven so tight that it's difficult to move the brace.

The next step is to assemble the base. With a small brush, I spread glue on one tenon at a time, then fit it in its mortise (photo 3-9). With a pipe clamp, I pull the legs tightly against the rails, then drill the joint to accept a pair of 1/4-in. dowels (photo 3-10). Centers for the dowels are 3/8 in. from the inner edge of the rail, and 3/8 in. from the top and bottom of the mortise. Bore the holes a full 3/4 in. deep, and drive 1-in.-long dowels into the joint as far as they'll go. They should protrude slightly so that you can sand them flush when the glue dries.

To complete the base, I glue and screw corner braces between the rails, just inside the legs (photo 3-11). These braces add strength and stability to the table, and also enable you to attach the top easily.

3-10 *After clamping each mortise-and-tenon joint tightly together, I drill it out with a 1/4-in. bit to accept a pair of dowel pegs.*

3-11 *Finish off the base by gluing and screwing a corner brace just inside each leg. By connecting the rails, these 4 braces strengthen the base assembly.*

Making the top

The finished dimensions of the broad center section of the table top are 19 in. by 42½ in. The "drop leaves," or moveable side sections, end up 12 in. wide and 42½ in. long. I use a combination of 1x6 and 1x8 ash boards to glue up all 3 sections. You should glue each piece up to be at least 1/2 in. wider and longer than its finished dimensions.

The table top deserves the best boards you've got, so go through your selection of ash and choose stock with similar grain and color. Once you've selected the wood, make sure that joining edges are straight, running the stock through the planer if necessary. Orient adjacent pieces so that the growth ring pattern (visible in the end grain of each piece) alternates up and down. Glued-up boards are more likely to warp if the growth ring pattern doesn't alternate.

I use 3 pipe clamps to glue up each top section. The 2 outermost clamps are positioned under the stock; the center clamp rests on top (photo 3-12). Spread glue evenly along joining edges and place wood clamping blocks between the metal clamping feet and the stock. Then tighten the clamps gradually, exerting even pressure across the full length of the work.

When the glue has dried, I go over the glue lines with a scraper, removing hardened glue so that the panel will rest flat as you square up the edges and cut it to final size. To do this, I use the panel cutter on the table saw because it handles large material more safely and accurately than the miter gauge. When all the pieces are cut, I give them a preliminary sanding, using the belt sander and a medium-grit sanding belt.

Now the drop-leaf edges can be milled in all 3 top pieces. Traditionally, these edges are designed to interlock in a curve-and-cove

3-12 The table top is glued up from 3 ash boards. Pipe clamps alternate over and under the stock to help keep clamping pressure even.

3-13 *The pin of the drop-leaf hinge fits in a 1/4-in.-wide groove cut in the underside of the top's center section. A piece of sandpaper, temporarily wedged in the drop-leaf joint, provides 1/16 in. of clearance between the pieces when the hinge is first screwed to the table.*

joint. The drop leaves get the cove and the center piece gets the curved edges. Both profiles are shown in drawing 3-F.

I use a 3/8-in. roundover bit to mill the long edges of the center piece. The bit's depth of cut is adjusted to leave a 3/16-in.-wide shoulder at the top edge of the curve. Once these edges are done, chuck a 3/8-in.-radius cove bit in the router and adjust its depth to mill a matching fit in the leaves. Be sure to test the cove bit's depth by cutting a sample edge in some scrap stock. Fine-tune the depth adjustment if necessary, then mill the inner edges of the drop leaves.

Attaching the hinges comes next. You'll need a pair of drop-leaf hinges for each side of the table. These hinges are made with one side (also called a "leaf") longer than the other, and it's the long side that's screwed to the top's drop leaf. I position the hinges 1/4 in. outside of where the legs will join the table. I don't mortise the hinges, but the hinge pin needs to rest in a short groove cut close to the edge of the center piece.

To cut the grooves for the pins, I chuck a 1/4-in., roundnose bit in the router and attach a fence to the router base. I adjust the fence so that it's 1/8 in. away from the bit; then I adjust the bit's depth of cut to 1/4 in. Finally, I turn the router on and tip the bit carefully into the wood. When I've made the groove long enough to hold the pin, I tip the bit free and turn off the router. If you haven't tried this technique with the router before, practice on some scrap stock before you work on your center piece.

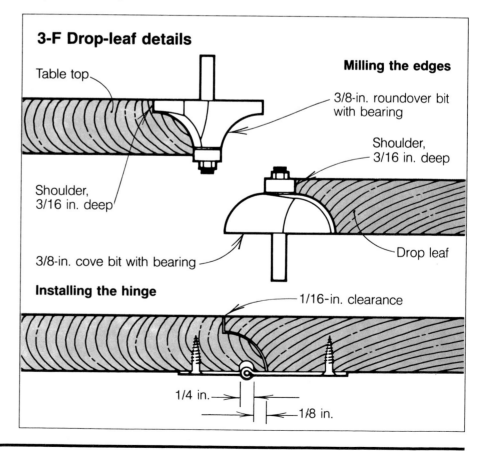

3-F Drop-leaf details

Table top

Milling the edges

3/8-in. roundover bit with bearing

Shoulder, 3/16 in. deep

Shoulder, 3/16 in. deep

3/8-in. cove bit with bearing

Drop leaf

Installing the hinge

1/16-in. clearance

1/4 in.

1/8 in.

Now the hinge can be screwed to the center section of the top. Pre-drill the screw holes, taking care not to drill all the way through the wood. To screw the hinge to the drop leaf, I insert a piece of sandpaper into the drop-leaf joint before pre-drilling and driving the screws (photo 3-13). This creates about 1/16 in. of clearance between the parts — enough room for coats of finish and also for normal wood movement that might cause a tighter joint to bind.

It's time to attach the top. I place it on the workbench, "good" side facing down. Then I center the base on the center section of the top, and drive a single 1 1/4-in. drywall screw through each corner brace and into the top (photo 3-14).

With the table turned rightside-up, I trace the curve of a quarter into the top's 4 outer corners, then sand to these lines with the belt sander. Using a 1/4-in. roundover bit in the router, I go over the top's edges to give the table a softer look and feel. Finally, I give the entire piece a thorough sanding in preparation for its finish. As with all tables, you should spend extra time smoothing the top, since it will be the most visible part of your table, and take the most use.

When it comes time to apply the finish to your table, it's smart to detach the base from the top and finish these parts separately. This way, you'll be able to give the underside of the table top the same finishing treatment as the good side. If you don't follow this strategy, the top pieces will absorb and release moisture unevenly. This can cause the wood to warp or crack.

3-14 It just takes 4 screws to attach the top. I use 1 1/4-in. drywall screws, driving 1 through each corner brace and into the center section of the top. Make sure the base is centered on the top before you fasten the 2 parts together.

Chapter 4

Blanket chest

Before central heating came along, blanket chests served a singular purpose. In the typical Colonial household, you'd find a blanket chest in every room, just at the foot of the bed. Today, chests like this one have many uses. They're still good for blankets, but they can just as easily hold toys, sleeping bags, and sweaters. And they're equally at home in the living room or hallway.

This chest has a very traditional frame-and-panel design. Historically, it's more sophisticated than the chests that were fashioned by using a single broad board for each side. The frame consists of vertical "stiles" and horizontal "rails," held together with mortise-and-tenon joints. At the corners of the chest, paired stiles join together to form legs. A center stile divides the front and back of the chest into two frames. Panels, each cut from a single board, fit into grooves that are milled along the inside edges of each frame. Unlike the glued joints of the frame, panels "float" in their grooves, so they can expand and contract freely in response to humidity changes. Because of this, frame-and-panel construction is inherently durable and stable over time.

The top of the chest swings open on a brass-plated piano hinge. The top is made from edge-glued boards, with a "breadboard-style" edge along each end. Apart from giving the top a fancier look, the breadboard edge provides good resistance to warping. The chest bottom is aromatic cedar, a traditional choice for chests and closets because its strong odor is a natural moth repellant. The tongue-and-groove cedar boards are installed over a base of 1/2-in.-thick plywood.

From the top down

Most of your time on this project will be spent cutting joints. The joinery details for this chest probably seem more complex than they are. With careful planning, you'll find that the construction process can be broken down into several basic joint-milling operations, first on the router table and then on the table saw. With a few different set-ups, you'll be milling many parts that match, either in size, or in joint dimensions.

Before the joinery begins, however, let's glue up the top. Choose clear, straight stock at least 41 in. long. Make sure that the edges to be joined are straight and square; then arrange the boards so their end grains show an alternating pattern of growth rings. Use four clamps to glue up the top— 2 clamps underneath and 2 on top. Once you've tightened the clamps, you can move the top out of the way to free up your bench for the work to come.

When the glue has cured, I cut the top to its finished length using a panel cutter, a jig that you can make to handle large stock on the table saw (see Introduction). To cut the tongue in the top's end-grain edges, I use a router with a rabbeting bit (photo 4-1). I like to use a carbide-tipped bit with a pilot bearing, but you can also use a high-speed steel bit with a pilot shaft. Adjust the bit's depth of cut so that the tongue will be about 1/4 in. thick; then mill a matching groove in the edge boards with a dado cutter on your table saw. Lift the front of each edge board free of the cutter before the dado penetrates the end. This way, the tongue-and-groove joint will remain hidden when viewed from the front of the chest (for more on this technique, see chapter 5 and photo 5-2).

4-1 For the top's breadboard-style edges, mill tongues using a router and a rabbeting bit. Adjust the bit's depth of cut so that after two passes on either side of the joint, a 1/4-in.-thick tongue remains.

4-A Major anatomy and dimensions

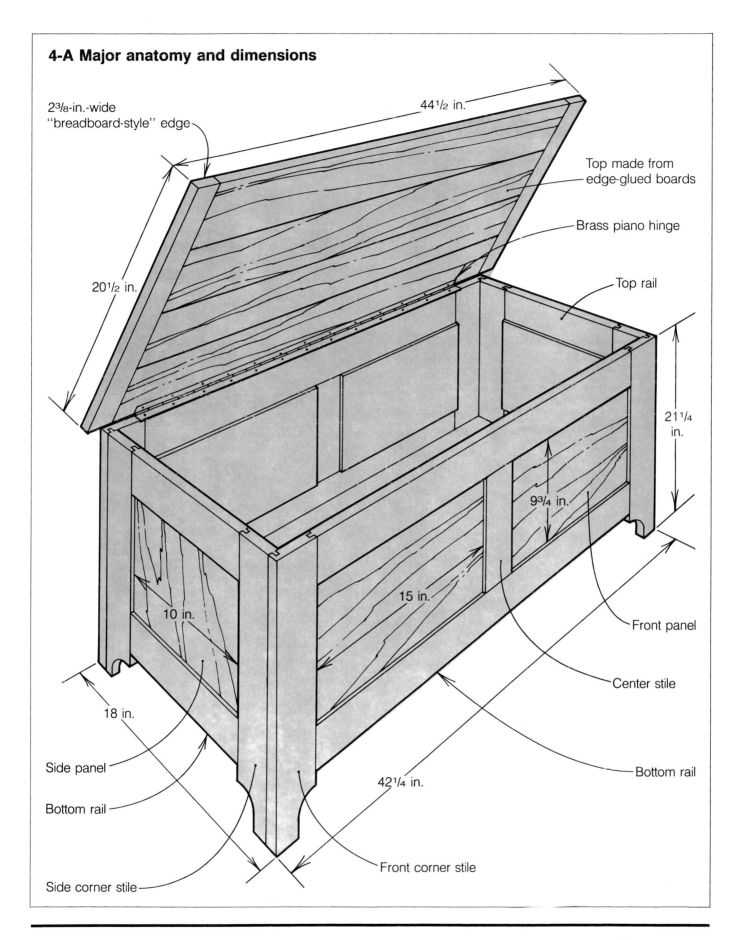

2³/₈-in.-wide "breadboard-style" edge

44¹/₂ in.

Top made from edge-glued boards

Brass piano hinge

20¹/₂ in.

Top rail

21¹/₄ in.

9³/₄ in.

Front panel

15 in.

Center stile

10 in.

18 in.

Bottom rail

Side panel

Bottom rail

42¹/₄ in.

Side corner stile

Front corner stile

4-2 A cut-off saw, equipped with finish-cutting blade and an adjustable stop, makes fast, precise work of cutting stiles and rails to finished length.

Get the parts together

Because this is a frame-and-panel design, parts can be grouped in sets. For example, there are 4 long rails — a pair for the front of the chest, and a pair for the back. Likewise, you'll need 2 pairs of short rails for the sides, and a pair of side panels. Four identical panels are required for the front and back of the chest. Don't start cutting joints until you've got a full set of stiles, rails and panels (see the parts list shown in the box at left).

Except for the side stiles and the upper back rail, all rails and stiles are 4 in. wide. Rip all this 4-in.-wide stock at the same time, using the same set-up on the table saw. When this is done, rip the side stiles to their finished width of 3⁵/₈ in. Then rip the top back rail to a finished width of 3⁷/₈ in. This rail needs to sit 1/8 in. below the top edges of the chest to provide clearance for the piano hinge.

The next step is to cut all stiles and rails to their finished lengths. A cut-off saw, with a fence extension and an adjustable stop, makes this repetitive work go quickly and accurately (photo 4-2). For example, after setting the stop up for a 21¹/₄-in. cut, you can cut all 8 of the long stiles. Only after these are cut will you re-adjust the stop for another series of repetitive cuts.

Grooves and mortises on the router table

You'll notice that the legs of this chest are actually corner stiles in the chest frame that extend below the bottom rails. I used a tongue-and-groove joint to connect the two stiles that make each leg. This joint runs the full length of leg. The front and rear stiles are milled with grooves, while the side stiles get the tongues (see drawing 4-B). It's a good idea to mill the grooves first. I did this work on the router table, using a 3/8-in. straight bit.

Use a carbide router bit if you can. Cutting long grooves builds up plenty of heat, and high-speed steel bits can lose their temper, become dull, and actually burn the wood. To set up the cut, raise bit height to a strong 3/8 in. ("Strong," in carpenter's parlance, translates to 1/32 in. more than the stated measurement.) Then adjust the router table's fence so that the 3/8-in.-wide groove will start 3/16 in. away from the outside edge of the stile. If your stiles are 3/4 in. thick, this 3/16-in. setback will make the corner flush where the two stiles meet. Run a test groove in scrap stock to make sure the groove is 3/16 in. away from the bit.

Once the set-up is right, you're ready to mill grooves in the 2 front stiles and the 2 rear ones. Move the stiles through the bit with firm, steady pressure, exerted both downward and against the fence (photo 4-3). Slow down your feed rate as the bit leaves the wood to avoid any tear-out that might mar the joint.

Without changing the router table set-up, you can now mill the mortises in all 8 corner stiles. All mortises are 3/8 in. wide and 3/8 in. deep. Let's mill the top mortises first. These start 3¹/₂ in. down from the top of each stile, and extend right through the top edge. (You can see these joints when you open the chest. Refer also to drawing 4-C.)

Feed the stiles top-first into the bit, with the face of the stile held firmly against the router table fence. Clamp a stop block to the fence exactly 3¹/₂ in. from the bit's leading edge (the edge that will enter the stock first). When you've fed the stile through the bit and it butts against the stop block, you've cut the full length of the mortise (photo 4-4). Test this set-up on scrap stock to make sure the stop block is positioned correctly.

Cut the mortises for the bottom rails next. These begin 4 in. up from the bottom of each leg, and extend only 3 in. To cut the lower mortises, you have to lower the leg down over the bit just where the bottom edge of the mortise begins. Make a mark on the fence 4 in. away from the bit's trailing edge. Keep the bottom of each stile even with this mark as you lower the stile down onto the bit. Clamp a stop block 3 in. down from this mark so that the stile bottom will butt

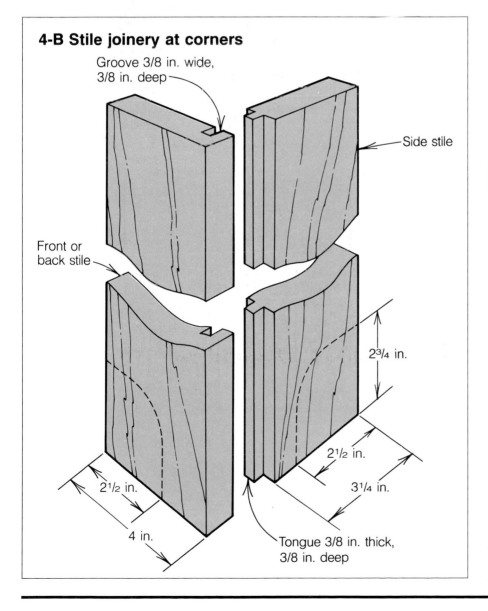

4-B Stile joinery at corners

Groove 3/8 in. wide, 3/8 in. deep

Side stile

Front or back stile

2³/4 in.

2¹/2 in.

2¹/2 in.

3¹/4 in.

4 in.

Tongue 3/8 in. thick, 3/8 in. deep

4-3 Groove the front and back stiles on the router table, using a 3/8-in. straight bit. Bit height is just over 3/8 in., and the fence should be set 3/16 in. away from the bit. Keep the bit and fence set up this way until you've milled all the grooves and all the mortises.

4-4 Clamp a stop block against the fence when milling the upper mortises. Locate the stop block so that when the stile's top edge butts against the stop block, the full 3½-in. length of the mortise will have been cut.

4-C Stile and rail joinery

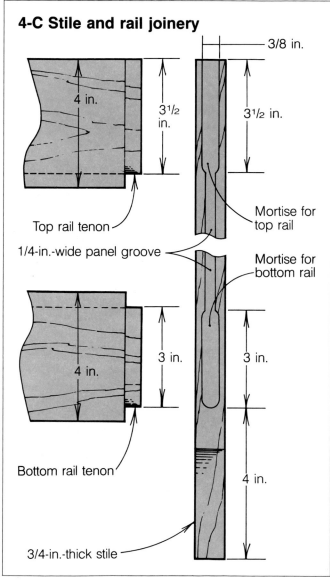

4 in.

3½ in.

3/8 in.

3½ in.

Top rail tenon

1/4-in.-wide panel groove

Mortise for top rail

Mortise for bottom rail

4 in.

3 in.

3 in.

4 in.

Bottom rail tenon

3/4-in.-thick stile

4-5 To cut the lower mortises, stiles must be firmly lowered down over the bit. The cut begins at the lower end of the mortise, and ends 3 in. later, when the bottom edge of the stile butts against a stop block clamped to the rip fence.

against it as the full 3-in. length of the mortise is cut. Again, test this set-up on scrap stock to make sure you'll be cutting the mortise in the right place on the stile. To mill the mortise, lower the stile onto the bit with slow, firm pressure. When you reach the full depth of the mortise, feed the stile forward until you hit the stop block; then carefully lift the stile free (see photo 4-5).

Curves, tongues and tenons

The legs are curved at the bottom to give the chest a lighter, more graceful appearance. I traced the curve by hand on one stile, cut it out on the bandsaw and then transferred it to the remaining stiles. It's easy to hand-trace the curve if you make a couple of right-angled layout lines at the bottom of a stile. As shown in drawing 4-B, the curve begins 2³/₄ in. up from the bottom, and ends 2¹/₂ in. from the inner edge of the stile.

Because I used a bandsaw with a 1/4-in. blade, I was able to clamp two stiles together and cut both at once (photo 4-6). If you don't have access to a bandsaw, these curves can be cut easily with a portable jigsaw or even a coping saw.

The tongues on the side stiles and all rail tenons are cut on the table saw. To make the best use of saw set-ups, I cut the "shoulders" for the tongues first. Then I switch to cutting tenon shoulders and trimming the tops and bottoms of the tenons. Finally, the tenon cheeks and the sides of the tongues are cut using the same set-up. This may sound confusing, but it isn't if you follow the step-by-step procedure described below.

First let's take care of the shoulder cuts for the tongues on the side stiles. These tongues are milled 3/8 in. thick and 3/8 in. deep to match the grooves in front and back stiles. Adjust the table saw so that the blade shows 3/16 in. above the table. Then adjust the rip fence so that it's exactly 3/8 in. away from the outside edge of the blade (the edge farthest away from the fence). Test this set-up on some scrap wood to make sure it's accurate. If it checks out, run the side stiles through the saw, holding the "tongue" edge of the stock against the rip fence. You'll have to flip each piece to make a pair of identical shoulder cuts (photo 4-7).

Now we'll switch to cutting the tenon shoulders on all the rails. Keep blade height at 3/16 in. Because the rails are long and narrow, you'll need to hold the rails against the miter gauge (set at 90 degrees) as you make the shoulder cuts. By clamping a gauge block to the rip fence, in front of the saw blade, you can adjust the rip fence so that this gauge block stops the end of the rail at exactly 3/8-in. tenon depth (see photo 4-8). This gauge block set-up is necessary because it's not safe to make a cut on the table saw with the stock running against both the rip gauge and the miter gauge. Make a pair of shoulder cuts in each end of the rail by flipping the stock. Repeat this operation for every rail tenon.

4-6 Curved stile bottoms can be cut two at a time, with a pair of stiles clamped together and run through a bandsaw. A portable jigsaw can also be used for this job.

Milling tongues and tenons

4-7 (top left) Set blade height to 3/16 in. and cut the tongue "shoulders" first, running the tongue edge of the stock against the rip fence. The fence should be set 3/8 in. away from the "outside" edge of the blade. Flip each side stile to make a pair of identical shoulder cuts.

4-8 (top) Now cut tenon shoulders with the blade at the same height. Clamp a gauge block to the rip fence as shown and adjust the fence so that the gauge block stops the end of the rail at 3/8-in. tenon depth. With rails held against the miter gauge (set at 90 degrees), make a pair of shoulder cuts in each rail end.

4-9 (bottom) Raise blade height to 1/2 in. and keep the gauge block in place to trim tenons to finished length. Holding the rails on edge against the miter gauge, "nibble" away the tenon top (or bottom) until the end of the tenon stops against the gauge block.

4-10 (bottom left) Cut tenon cheeks by running rails vertically through the blade, with the face of the rail held against the rip fence. Blade height should be 3/8 in., and the fence should be 9/16 in. away from the the blade. Make two passes with each rail end. Then use the same set-up and technique to cut the sides of the tongues.

Tenons in all bottom rails have to be cut back 1/2 in. top and bottom, to a finished length of 3 in. Tenons in all top rails are trimmed back 1/2 in. on the bottom only (see drawing 4-C). You can do this trimming by adjusting blade height to 1/2 in. Keep the same rip fence and gauge block set-up. Holding the rails horizontally, on edge against the miter gauge, "nibble" away the tenon top (or bottom) until the end of the tenon stops against the gauge block (photo 4-9). Repeat this operation until all tenon trimming is complete.

Now I set up the saw a little differently to cut the tenon cheeks and finish off the sides of the tongues. Raise blade height to 3/8 in. and set the rip fence 9/16 in. away from the outside edge of the blade. Each tongue and each tenon edge has to be run twice through the blade, holding one face of the stock against the rip fence, then the other (photo 4-10). Don't run your stiles or rails through this set-up until you've milled a sample tenon and test-fitted it in a mortise. You might need to adjust the rip fence to make the tenons (and tongues) slightly thinner or thicker. Finally, use a sharp utility knife to round off tenon ends that need to fit into mortises with rounded tops or bottoms.

Remember the techniques described above, because you'll need to repeat them to cut tenons in the center stiles. The only difference is that these tenons are just 1/4 in. thick and 3/8 in. deep. Instead of fitting into separate 3/8-in.-wide mortises, these tenons fit into the panel groove cut in top and bottom rails, so they're only 1/4 in. thick.

Panel grooves and panels

The final operation in preparing the frame of the chest is to mill panel grooves in stiles and rails. These grooves are 1/4 in. wide and 3/8 in. deep, and I mill them using a dado cutter in the table saw. Set the dado to 1/4-in. width, and raise the cutter 3/8 in. above the table. Now set the rip fence 1/4 in. away from the cutter. Test this set-up on a scrap piece of 3/4-in.-thick stock to make sure the groove is centered exactly.

The panel grooves are cut along the "inside" edges of all rails, and between the top and bottom mortises of all stiles. Grooving the rails is fairly straightforward. The stiles should be run top-first through the cutter, so that the dado will start to cut at the bottom of the upper mortise. Lift the stile free before the dado cutter penetrates beyond the bottom of the lower mortise.

The frame is now basically complete. Dry-fit the frame together, one side at a time. If you haven't cut and milled the two center stiles, now is the time to do it. Once these are done and test-fitted, you can measure the framed openings and cut the panels to fit in them.

I cut the panels from 1x12 pine boards. You'll notice that front and back panels have their grains running horizontally, while side panel grain runs vertically. This arrangement seems to look best. Each panel is rabbeted on all four sides, and "floats" in the frame's 1/4-in.-wide grooves. The grooves are 3/8 in. deep, but it's not a good idea to size the panels 3/4 in. larger than the frame openings. Instead, I size each panel 1/2 in. larger than its frame opening. This creates a 1/8-in. air space around all panel edges, allowing the panel to expand without buckling or cracking the frame (see photo 4-13).

When you've cut all the panels to size, you can rabbet their edges on the table saw. The rabbet is 1/4 in. thick and 3/8 in. deep. As when milling the tenons, I cut the shoulders first on the table saw, then the cheeks (photo 4-11). As a finishing touch, adjust the blade to cut a 45-degree bevel and bevel the inside edges of the panels (photo 4-12). These edges will be exposed inside the chest. Without the bevel, they look awkward and present sharp angles that can snag clothes and other stored items.

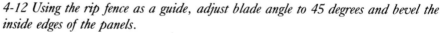

4-12 Using the rip fence as a guide, adjust blade angle to 45 degrees and bevel the inside edges of the panels.

4-11 Panels must be rabbeted on all edges to fit into the grooved frame. Each 1/4-in.-thick, 3/8-in.-deep rabbet can be cut in two passes on the table saw. Cut the shoulders first, then the cheeks, as shown above.

4-13 The center stile is grooved to hold two panels and tenoned to fit into rail grooves. The panels aren't glued in place, but "float" in the grooved frame, with about 1/8 in. allowed for expansion around all four panel edges.

Assembly

Give the outside face of each panel a thorough sanding now, because
it's more trouble to sand in a panel's corners after it's inside the frame.
Now is also the time to recruit a helper. It's difficult to glue up the
front and back of the chest without an extra pair of hands. Smear glue
on the tenons and tenon shoulders only. Use two clamps per side,
positioned along the rails. As you glue and clamp each side, check the
inside faces of the panels to make sure they're centered in their
frames. A tiny spot of glue can lock a panel off-center in its frame,
possibly causing problems later on when the panel shrinks or expands.
When gluing up the back of the chest, remember that the top rail has
to sit 1/8 in. below the top edges of the rear stiles to allow for the
thickness of the piano hinge.

Before gluing the sides to each other, sand the panels and frames
that will face inside. Then glue and screw down the cleats that will

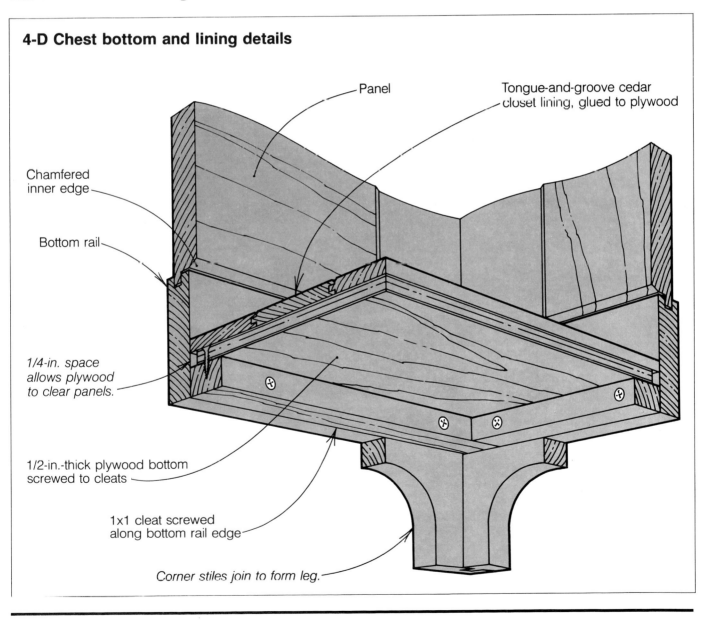

4-D Chest bottom and lining details

Panel

Tongue-and-groove cedar
closet lining, glued to plywood

Chamfered
inner edge

Bottom rail

1/4-in. space
allows plywood
to clear panels.

1/2-in.-thick plywood bottom
screwed to cleats

1x1 cleat screwed
along bottom rail edge

Corner stiles join to form leg.

support the bottom of the chest. I cut these from 1x1 stock, and attach them with 1¼-in. drywall screws. The bottom edges of the cleats should be flush with the bottom edges of the lower rails, as shown in drawing 4-D.

Now it's finally time to glue the chest sides together. Spread glue on the tongues that run the length of each side stile, then assemble the tongue-and-groove joints that make each leg. Make sure the top edges of the chest's sides are flush with each other, and check the chest for square. If necessary, install a temporary diagonal brace across the bottom (or top) of the chest to keep it square until the glue cures. You'll need four clamps to pull the joints tight (photo 4-14).

Top and bottom

The bottom of the chest is a single piece of 1/2-in. plywood. Screwed to the cleats on the bottom rails, the plywood lends rigidity to the chest and also provides a base for the aromatic cedar lining (see drawing 4-D). Inside the chest, the panels protrude 1/4 in. beyond the frame. Because of this, you need to adjust the plywood's dimensions slightly to allow this bottom piece to clear the panels as you install it. To get the finished dimensions of the plywood, I subtract 1/8 in. from the inside width of the chest, measured from front rail to back rail. I also subtract 1/2 in. from the inside length of the chest, measured from side rail to side rail.

4-14 Glue up each side separately, then assemble the chest by gluing and clamping the tongue-and-groove joints at the corners. Use four clamps, positioned across the side rails. If necessary, brace the chest square until the glue cures.

4-15 The piano hinge extends the full length of the top back rail, including tenons. After fastening the hinge to the rail, prop the chest up on its back, position the top, and screw the free side of the hinge in place. Use an awl to start piano hinge screws.

After you've screwed the plywood in place, install the cedar boards by gluing them to the bottom with panel adhesive. These tongue-and-groove boards come in random lengths, and I installed them parallel with the front and back of the chest. Glue down the first row with the grooved edge of the boards butting against the front or back rail. In order to fit the last row in place, you might have to saw off the bottom edge of the groove so that this board can slip in over the tongue on the previous row.

The top goes on last. It swings on a piano hinge that's screwed to the top edge of the back rail. Using a fine-toothed crosscut saw, trim back the tops of the mortises at the back of the chest so that the piano hinge can lie flat along the full length of the top rail, including tenons (see photo 4-15). After cutting the piano hinge to its finished size (in my chest, 35 in.), screw the hinge to the chest first. Instead of drilling pilot holes for the piano hinge's many screws, I start the screws by making shallow holes with an awl.

When the hinge is fastened to the back rail, put the chest on its back, propped about 3/4 in. off the floor. Position the top close to the free side, or "leaf," of the piano hinge, with its back edge showing an even overlap on both sides of the chest. Now use an awl and screwdriver to attach the hinge to the top.

Now that the blanket chest is complete, it deserves a thorough sanding before you apply the finish. A clear varnish or oil finish will show off the grain nicely, but chests like this one were often painted. No matter what finish you use, be sure to seal the inside of the chest when you finish the outside. There's no need to apply any finish on the cedar lining.

Chapter 5

Bedside table

Inspired by a traditional Shaker design, this bedside table is just as useful in other locations. It makes a nice side table for a living room couch; or it might grace a hallway, holding a vase of flowers beneath a window.

Good proportions give this small table its pleasing lines (drawing 5-A). The legs are tapered, and on all four sides the rails are inset slightly, creating a delicate reveal. The top is made from edge-glued pine boards. It overhangs on all sides and is built "breadboard-style," with the end grain along both sides covered by a narrow edge board. This treatment does more than just make the top look good. It also helps to protect the top from warping due to changing moisture and humidity conditions.

I made this table from clear pine, but you might consider substituting a hardwood like oak, walnut or poplar. The project is small enough so that hardwood's extra expense would be negligible.

Order of work
When making a table, it's smart to glue up the top first. While the glue sets up, you can start making other parts. Make the legs next, then cut the rails to size. Cut mortises and tenons and assemble the frame. After fastening the top in place, you can install drawer supports and build the drawer.

Making the top
The top for this table is made from edge-glued boards, like many larger table tops. My preference when gluing up any table top is to use a number of narrow boards instead of just a few wide boards. Wide boards are far more prone to warping, regardless of how flat they are when you glue them up.

Select your boards carefully. Avoid warped stock, and boards that aren't exactly the same thickness. The top is the most noticeable part of this table, so be sure that the boards used to make it have similar grain characteristics. It won't look good if one board has knots or dark sapwood while the others don't. Lay your stock out on the bench and pick the boards that give the most consistent appearance.

You don't have to square the end-grain edges of the boards before gluing up, but you do have to make sure that all edges to be glued are perfectly flat and square. Plane edges straight if you have to, until you're sure of good joints.

Pipe clamps are ideal for gluing boards edge-to-edge. For best results, use three clamps for this top —two positioned underneath the boards and one on top. Protect your workbench from glue squeeze-out by laying several layers of newspaper under the lower clamps (photo 5-1).

Use clamping blocks between the stock and the clamping feet. After gluing the edges and placing the boards on the lower pair of clamps, tighten these clamps gradually and evenly. You can judge the evenness of clamping pressure by the evenness of glue squeeze-out. Position the top bar clamp in between the two lower ones, and tighten it last. Resist the urge to apply extreme clamping pressure. Pipe clamps are capable of applying far more pressure than is necessary for a good joint, and overtightening can cause flat boards to bow needlessly.

Once the glue has cured, remove the clamps by releasing pressure gradually and evenly, just the way you applied it. Use a paint scraper to remove any beads of glue that have hardened where edges join. Now you can rip the workpiece to its finished width of 16 in.

The next step is to square up the stock by crosscutting the glued-up boards. The easiest way to do this is to use the panel-cutting jig on the table saw. When crosscutting the top, remember that its finished length (including the "breadboard" edges) will be 19½ in. If you take into account the 2-in.-wide edging and the 1/2-in.-long tongue that needs to be milled into the end grain of the boards, this gives you a finished length of 16½ in. for the crosscut stock.

For the sake of appearance, the tongue-and-groove joint in each 2-in.-wide breadboard edge is hidden in this table top. I mill the tongue on the table saw, cutting the "shoulders" first, and then the "cheeks." The technique is the same one I use for cutting tenons in the rails (see photos 5-6 — 5-9).

To mill the groove in the edge boards, I also use the table saw, but with a dado head instead of a saw blade. Set the dado to cut a groove 1/4 in. wide and 9/16 in. deep. In order to stop the groove short of the end grain, you have to lower the edge board over the dado head and then lift it clear before the cutterhead penetrates the other end of the board. This is careful work, and it's smart to mill a practice groove in scrap 1x stock before running your edge stock through. Brace the stock firmly against the saw fence, and use pencil marks on the saw

5-1 Use three pipe clamps to glue up the top, two underneath and one on top. Tighten the lower clamps first, using glue squeeze-out to gauge the evenness of clamping pressure.

5-A Major anatomy and dimensions

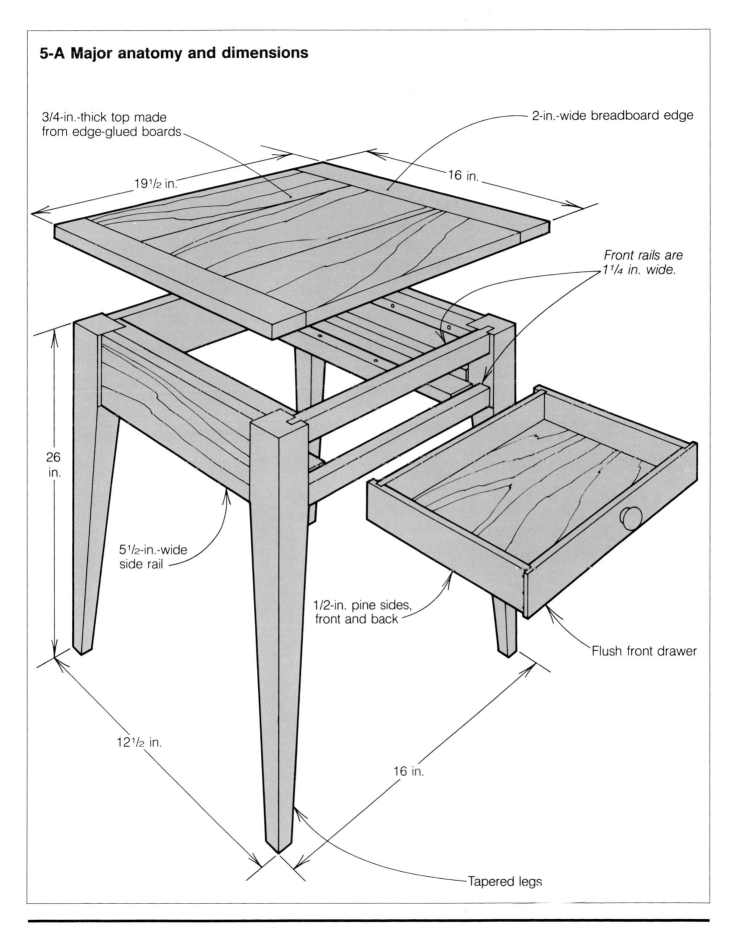

3/4-in.-thick top made from edge-glued boards

2-in.-wide breadboard edge

19½ in.

16 in.

Front rails are 1¼ in. wide.

26 in.

5½-in.-wide side rail

1/2-in. pine sides, front and back

Flush front drawer

12½ in.

16 in.

Tapered legs

5-2 *"Breadboard-style" edges cover the end grain of the glued-up boards and give the top a finer look. Each 2-in.-wide edge piece joins the top with a hidden tongue-and-groove joint that can be cut on the table saw. Glue and clamp these edges to the top.*

table to indicate where the cutter penetrates the table surface.

To make the joint fit, trim the tongue back on all four corners of the top (see photo 5-2). Test-fit the joint, trim the tongue more if necessary, then glue and clamp the breadboard edges. Once the glue has cured, give the top a thorough sanding. As the most noticeable part of the table, the top deserves a good smoothing. Be careful not to sand across the grain when sanding near the breadboard edges. Finally, ease the edges of the finished top with some fine sandpaper to remove any sharp corners. Now set the top aside until you've built the frame.

Making the legs

Make the legs from clear, straight-grained stock. Small, tight knots are acceptable for other parts of the table, but legs—especially tapered ones—have to be knot-free for strength and appearance.

The finished length of the legs is 26 in. In cross section, they measure 1⁹/₁₆ in. square. Because I couldn't find any solid leg stock, I made each leg by gluing a pair of 3/4-in.-thick boards together. By making the boards 1³/₄ in. wide, I left room for squaring up the legs after the glued cured. In cross section, it's fine for these legs to be slightly larger or smaller than 1⁹/₁₆ in., as long as they're identical and square. Otherwise, the table's frame won't come out square.

The two inside faces of each leg are tapered. The taper starts 7 in. down from the top of the leg, 1¹/₂ in. below the rail. The degree of taper is almost a full inch over 19 in. of length, leaving a 3/4-in. square at the bottom of the leg. With a simple taper jig designed to be used on your table saw, it's easy to cut tapers quickly and accurately (see sidebar).

After you've tapered all the legs, smooth all leg surfaces to remove saw marks and other irregularities. I run the legs through a jointer, but you could also use an orbital sander. It's easier to smooth leg surfaces now than it will be after the table's frame is together. Sanding by hand, ease all edges on the legs to remove sharp corners.

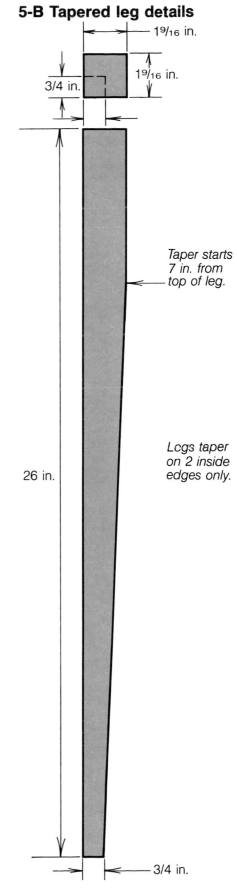

How to use a taper jig

Tapered legs, even delicate ones, aren't difficult to cut precisely if you have a taper jig to use with your table saw. A good jig won't take long to make, and the materials cost next to nothing. I made mine from 2 straight boards 3/4 in. thick, 3 in. wide and 30 in. long. The boards are hinged together at one end and connected at the other end with a simple sliding mechanism that can be adjusted and clamped with a thumbscrew. A stop at the back of the jig holds the back end of the workpiece.

It's easy to adjust the jig to cut different tapers, but first you have to lay out the taper on the workpiece. Use a square to extend the layout lines for the taper down the front and back edges of the stock. Now, with the straight side of the jig positioned against the rip fence, adjust the "swinging" side of the jig so that the layout lines on the workpiece align with the miter gauge guide slot in the saw table (photo 5-3). The workpiece should rest against a stop at the back of the taper jig as you make this adjustment.

To set up the cut after the jig is adjusted, you'll have to adjust the rip fence so that the saw blade lines up with the tapered layout lines on the workpiece. To make the tapered cut, both the jig and the workpiece must move together, riding against the rip fence (photo 5-4). Make the cut carefully, moving the jig and workpiece with slow, firm pressure. Always make a test taper in scrap before running good wood through the saw.

5-3 To adjust the degree of taper on the jig, hold the straight side of the jig against the rip fence, and adjust the swinging side until the layout lines on the stock are parallel with the saw blade.

5-4 Make the tapered cut by carefully moving the jig and the workpiece together through the saw blade. The straight side of the jig rides against the rip fence; the adjustable side holds the workpiece.

Leg mortises using a router and router table

The table's legs are connected with rails on all four sides. Legs and rails form the overall structure of the table, so the joinery has to be precise and strong. I chose mortise-and-tenon joints between legs and rails. I cut the mortises using a router, mounted in a router table. All the tenons were cut on the table saw.

Drawing 5-C shows the size and layout of the joints. All tenons are 1/2 in. wide and 1/2 in. long. Mortises in the legs are 1/2 in. wide and just over 1/2 in. deep (9/16 in.) to ensure clearance when clamping the joints tight. Instead of being flush with the outside faces of the legs, the rails are set back 1/8 in. on all four sides. This is a small but significant detail, because it creates a tiny shadow line that contributes to the delicacy of the piece.

A router table is a very worthwhile accessory. Coupled with your router, you've got a tool that performs like shaper, at a fraction of a shaper's cost. Let's cut the mortises in the legs first. Chuck a 1/2-in. straight bit in the router, and adjust the router's depth of cut from below so that 9/16 in. of bit shows above the table surface.

Carefully pencil in the layout lines on each leg, marking exactly where each mortise is located. Only the tapered leg sides receive mortises, which are cut 1/4 in. away from the outside face of the leg. It's easy to mismark and miscut these joints, so check everything twice. Use a square to extend mortise layout lines around to an

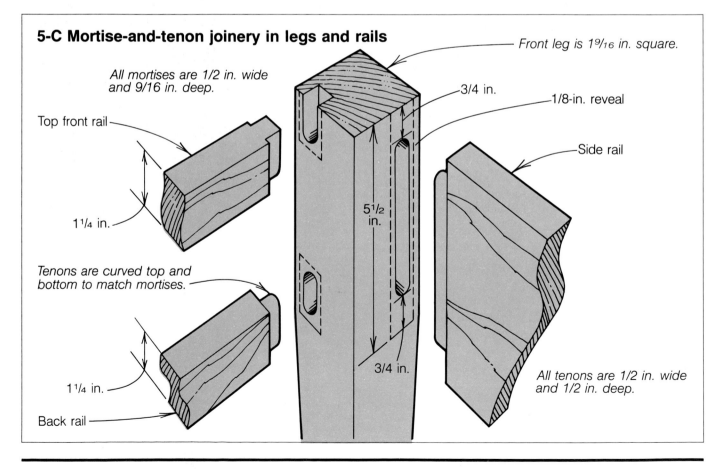

5-C Mortise-and-tenon joinery in legs and rails

Front leg is 1⁹/₁₆ in. square.

All mortises are 1/2 in. wide and 9/16 in. deep.

Top front rail

3/4 in.

1/8-in. reveal

Side rail

1¹/₄ in.

5¹/₂ in.

Tenons are curved top and bottom to match mortises.

1¹/₄ in.

Back rail

3/4 in.

All tenons are 1/2 in. wide and 1/2 in. deep.

5-5 To cut the leg mortises on the router table, legs must be held against the fence and carefully lowered over the router bit, then moved through the full length of the mortise and lifted clear.

adjacent face of the leg, and mark the bit's width of cut on the router table, penciling on a piece of tape stuck to the table, if necessary. These lines enable you to "see" the mortise layout and the bit, even though both will be hidden once you start cutting each joint. Now adjust the router table's fence so that the bit will cut exactly within the mortise layout.

Except for the top-most mortises in the front legs, all mortises must be cut by lowering the the leg down over the bit, using the fence as a guide (photo 5-5). This is tricky, and requires a firm hold on the stock. Make sure that your router table is firmly anchored so that there's no possibility of it shifting as you work. Mill the mortises slowly, using steady, even pressure.

Cutting tenons on the table saw

Prepare the side and back rails by first ripping them to their finished width of 5 1/2 in. The upper and lower front rails are only 1 1/4 in. wide. Instead of tenoning these rails separately, mill the tenons in a single, wider piece of wood and then rip the thin rails out. Cut all rail stock to finished length, allowing for 1/2-in.-long tenons at each end.

When using the table saw to cut tenons, I cut the shoulders first by running the rails face-down through the saw. The miter gauge is set at 90 degrees, blade height is 1/8 in. and the rip fence is set 1/2 in. away from the "outside" edge of the blade (the blade edge farthest from the rip fence), as shown in photo 5-6. Before you run rail stock through this set-up, test it out on a scrap piece.

The next step is to cut the tops and bottoms of the tenons on side and back rails. While these rails are 5 1/2 in. wide, their tenons are just

5-6 *Make the tenons' shoulder cuts first, with the blade set 1/8 in. above the table and the rip fence set 1/2 in. away from the outside edge of the blade. Run rails against the rip fence and the miter gauge, with the gauge set at 90 degrees.*

5-7 *Cut off the top and bottom of each tenon with the blade set at 1/2-in. height, and the rip fence 3/4 in. from the outside edge of the blade. Move the rails vertically through the saw, making successive passes to "nibble" the waste from the top and bottom of each tenon.*

5-8 *Cut the tenon cheeks last. Set the blade slightly less than 1/2 in. above the table. Each tenon requires two cheek cuts, with the rails held vertically against the rip fence. Set the fence so that tenon thickness is exactly 1/2 in. after two passes.*

4 in. from top to bottom. I set the saw up with the blade showing 1/2 in. above the table and the rip fence 3/4 in. away from the outside edge of the blade. Run the rails vertically through the saw, first cutting 3/4 in. off the tenon and then "nibbling" off the remainder by moving the long edge of the board away from the rip fence (photo 5-7). Repeat this operation until you've trimmed all tenons top and bottom. Note: Tenons on the thin front rails require a very slight trimming that can be done easily with a sharp utility knife.

To cut the tenon cheeks, set blade height just shy of 1/2 in. You'll be running the rails vertically through the saw, this time with the face of the stock held against the rip fence. Flopping each board will give you the two cheek cuts required for each tenon (photo 5-8). Set up the rip fence so that after both cuts, you'll have a 1/2-in.-thick tenon. Test your set-up on a scrap piece and keep adjusting the rip fence until the tenon thickness is exact. Once all the tenons are done, give each rail a thorough sanding.

Assembly

In order for rail tenons to fit into leg mortises, you'll have to round off the tops and bottoms of tenons. I use a sharp utility knife for this work (photo 5-9). Once this is done, you can test-fit the legs and rails. If you've cut your joints well, the table frame should hold together on its own. Now take everything apart, spread glue on the joints, and reassemble—this time for good. Crossing clamps, with clamp force transferred, via blocks, to legs, should snug up all joints (photo 5-10). As you tighten the clamps, test the frame at rail height with a framing square. If necessary, nail a temporary diagonal brace across the top of the table to keep rails and legs square with each other until the glue cures.

The top is attached from below, to keep the screws that hold it in place out of sight (drawing 5-D). Using 2-in. drywall screws, fasten 3/4-in.-thick by 1 1/2-in.-wide cleats against both side rails. The top face of each cleat should be flush with the top edge of its side rail.

To attach the top, first set it "good" side down on a protective work surface. Center the rail and leg framework on the top so that the overlap is divided evenly. Now attach the frame to the top by driving 1 1/4-in. screws through the cleats and into the top. Use only 3 evenly spaced screws per cleat. A table top this small shouldn't expand or contract enough to strain against the screws.

Drawer guides and drawer construction

Drawing 5-D also shows how the drawer guides for this table are installed. The two main drawer guides are a pair of simple, L-shaped supports that are screwed to the side rails. Make each support by joining together two lengths of 1x stock. Position each support so that the horizontal surface, where the drawer bottom will ride, is 1/16 in. above the top edge of the bottom rail. This will give proper clearance

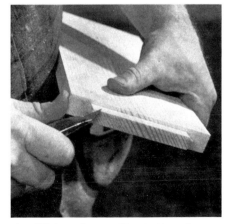

5-9 With a sharp utility knife, trim a rough curve into the top and bottom of each tenon. This should give the tenon a snug fit in its mortise, which is curved top and bottom from the router bit used to cut it.

5-10 *Dry-fit the rails and legs, and trim mortises or tenons as necessary for a good fit. Then glue and clamp the frame together. Test the rails and legs for squareness. If necessary, install a temporary brace to hold the frame square until the glue cures.*

for the drawer to operate freely. A third drawer guide, ripped to the same 1¼-in. width as the front rails, should be screwed to the underside of the top, right down the middle from front to back. This guide prevents the back of the drawer from tipping up as the drawer is opened and closed.

To make the drawer itself, I used 1/2-in.-thick pine for sides, back and front. Alternately, you could use a good grade of 1/2-in.-thick plywood for back and sides, since these parts won't be seen unless the drawer is opened. Don't use anything but solid wood for the front.

This drawer is small enough to rely on glue and fairly simple joints for strength. As shown in drawing 5-E, the 1/4-in. plywood bottom is held in a groove cut in the sides and front of the drawer. The bottom runs under the back, so the back is only as wide as the finished depth of the drawer. The back is dadoed into the sides. The front is rabbeted to hold the sides, with an extra 1/8 in. added to the width of each rabbet to ensure smooth closure (photo 5-11).

When sizing the drawer, keep in mind that the finished width from side to side should be 1/8 in. less than the distance between the side drawer guides. Finished length (from front to back) should be 1/16 in. less than the clearance allowed between front and back rails. And the dimensions of the drawer front should be 1/8 in. less than the measurements of the opening. Ideally, when the drawer is closed, an even 1/16 in. of clearance space should appear around all four edges of the drawer front.

Assemble the drawer with glue and 1¼-in. wire brads (photo 5-12). By crossing diagonals from each corner of the front, you can locate the center of the drawer so that you can drill out for the knob. To make the drawer slide in and out freely, wax the bottom edges of the sides.

5-11 *To glue up the drawer, first fasten the back to the sides. Then slide the bottom into slots cut in sides and front.*

5-12 *Glue the front to the sides amd nail through the sides into the shoulders of the rabbets, using 1¼-in. brads.*

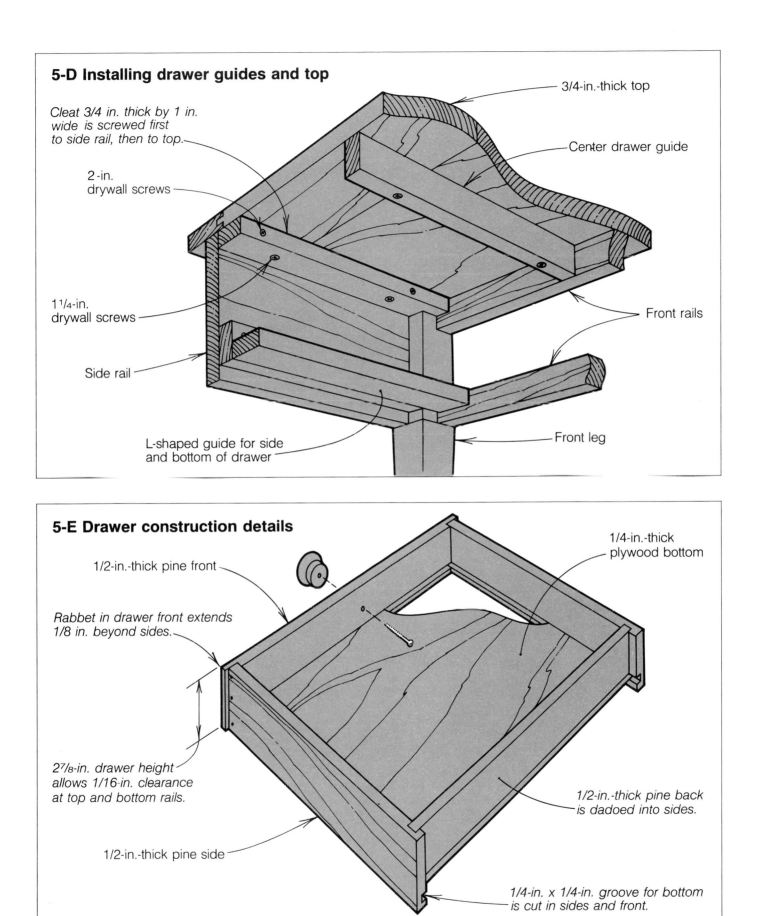

5-D Installing drawer guides and top

Cleat 3/4 in. thick by 1 in. wide is screwed first to side rail, then to top.

2-in. drywall screws

1 1/4-in. drywall screws

Side rail

L-shaped guide for side and bottom of drawer

3/4-in.-thick top

Center drawer guide

Front rails

Front leg

5-E Drawer construction details

1/2-in.-thick pine front

Rabbet in drawer front extends 1/8 in. beyond sides.

2 7/8-in. drawer height allows 1/16-in. clearance at top and bottom rails.

1/2-in.-thick pine side

1/4-in.-thick plywood bottom

1/2-in.-thick pine back is dadoed into sides.

1/4-in. x 1/4-in. groove for bottom is cut in sides and front.

Chapter 6

Bathroom vanity

The bathroom is a difficult place for cabinetry to survive. Subjected daily to standing water and high humidity, bathroom cabinets need replacing more often than built-ins located in other parts of the house. If it's time to upgrade your bathroom, you might consider making your own vanity, or base cabinet, instead of buying one from a home center or building supply outlet. I like the design of this vanity because it combines traditional joinery with the durability and clean look of plastic laminate. It's a nice companion for the medicine cabinet featured in chapter 1. With a dark laminate top, this cabinet would do well as a bar or sideboard. Installing the sink is optional.

There are a few details that set my design apart from many factory-made cabinets. First of all, this cabinet has sides that are solid wood instead of plywood or veneered particleboard. Doors are traditional frame-and-panel construction, with raised panels facing inside rather than outside. Instead of a laminate edge, the countertop on my vanity is edged in oak, with a chamfer where the laminate meets the wood. There's no "toe-kick," or floor-level recess, in my design. The overhang near the top of this cabinet takes its place, allowing you to step up comfortably against the edge of the countertop.

I've made my cabinet several inches higher than standard base cabinets. With a countertop height of 34 in., there's less bending over to be done when using the sink. The taller design is much more comfortable for me, but you can adjust the height of your vanity to suit your particular needs. Joinery is a final difference in my vanity. The base trim, the overhang and the top edge trim all have dovetailed joints at their corners.

Oak sides and pine frames

The sides of the vanity are 3/4-in.-thick oak. To make each side, I glue up a pair of 1x10 oak boards. This gives me a rough width of about 18 1/2 in. As soon as the glue has set, I square up the sides and cut them to their finished size of 18 1/4 in. by 32 1/2 in. Rabbeting the sides is the next step. On the table saw, I adjust the dado head for a 3/4-in.-wide cut, and raise the cutter 3/8 in. above the table. Then I position a wood auxiliary fence against the right side of the cutter. By running the top edge of each side against this fence and through the dado cutter, I mill a rabbet 3/4 in. wide and 3/8 in. deep (photo 6-1). While you've got this set-up, rabbet the top edges of the 2 side extension pieces. These small parts are eventually glued to the sides (see drawing 6-B), but they have to be cut and milled separately.

Now I rabbet the back edge of each side to hold the 1/4-in.-thick back of the vanity. To set up this cut (which is 3/8 in. wide and 3/8 in. deep), all you have to do is move the table saw's auxiliary fence 3/8 in. over the dado cutter. Run the back edge of each side against the fence and through the cutter. This completes the sides.

Two pine frames are joined to the sides. The top frame fits into the rabbeted top edges of the sides, and is made from 4 pieces of pine that are 3/4 in. thick and 2 in. wide. The outside dimensions of this frame should be 20 7/8 in. by 35 1/4 in. The front and back frame members are grooved to accept tongues milled in side frame members. Both types of joints are easy to mill on the table saw, using the dado head (see chapter 9: photos 9-1 and 9-2).

6-1 Rabbet the top edge of each vanity side using a wood auxiliary fence positioned against the dado cutter. Cutter height is 3/8 in. and width is 3/4 in.

6-A Major anatomy and dimensions

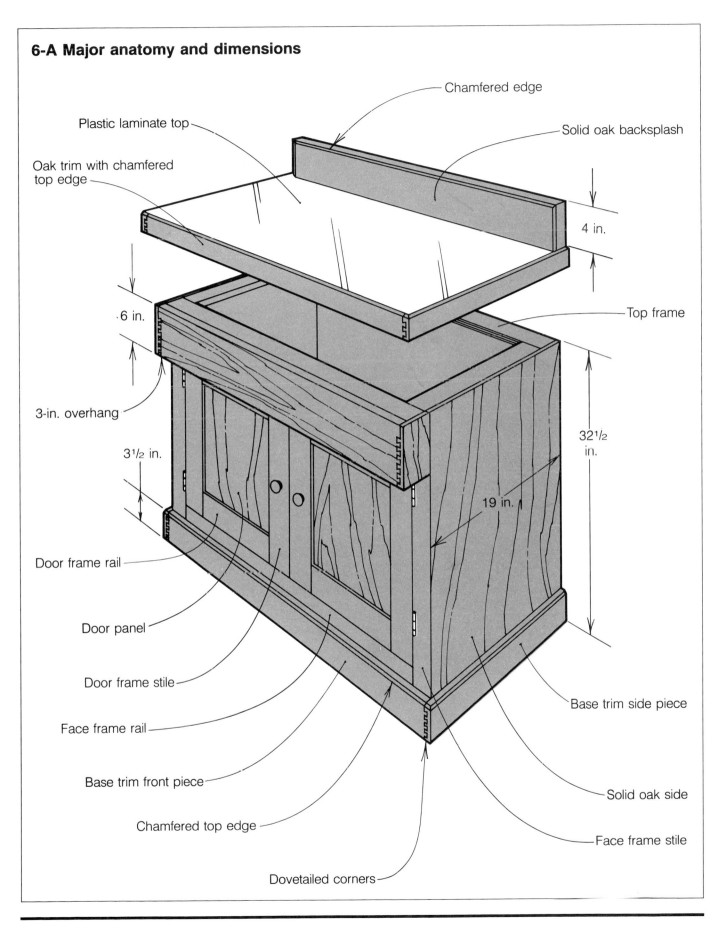

Chamfered edge

Plastic laminate top

Solid oak backsplash

Oak trim with chamfered top edge

4 in.

.6 in.

Top frame

3-in. overhang

3½ in.

32½ in.

19 in.

Door frame rail

Door panel

Door frame stile

Base trim side piece

Face frame rail

Solid oak side

Base trim front piece

Chamfered top edge

Face frame stile

Dovetailed corners

The bottom frame is designed to stand on edge, with its 4¼-in.-wide ends glued and screwed to the sides. Butt joints are fine for assembling the 4 pieces of this frame, but they should be glued and screwed together. Finished outside dimensions of this frame are 17⅞ in. by 34½ in.

Now the frames can be glued and screwed to the sides. The top frame should extend 3¾ in. beyond the sides' front edges (to hold the extension pieces). The front of the bottom frame should be flush with the front edge of each side. I glue all the joints between frames and sides, and pull them together with 1¼-in. drywall screws (photo 6-2). All screws should be driven from inside the vanity so that they don't show when the project is complete.

To complete the "carcase," or body of the vanity, install the bottom shelf and the back. I glue and nail the 3/4-in.-thick plywood shelf to the top edges of the bottom frame, using 6d finish nails (photo 6-3). Before you install the back, it's a good idea to fasten a 1x3 or 1x4 cleat underneath the back frame member at the back of the vanity. The cleat gives you something solid to screw through when you anchor the finished vanity to the wall. The 1/4-in.-thick plywood back fits in the rabbeted sides and against the back frame members. Before you glue and nail the back in place (I use 4d box nails), make sure the carcase is square.

6-2 Glue and screw the top and bottom frames to one side, then the other. The top frame should extend 3¾ in. beyond the sides' front edges.

6-3 The bottom shelf is 3/4-in.-thick, exterior-grade plywood. Fasten it to the top of the lower frame with glue and 6d finish nails.

Adding the overhang

In the finished vanity, the overhang is 6 in. high, and extends 3 in. beyond the face frame and doors below it. There are just 3 parts to the overhang, but they have to be made carefully because of the dovetailed joints at the corners. Because of the rabbet milled along the top edge of each side extension piece, the dovetails can't extend all the way up the corner. Instead, the top $1^3/8$ in. of the joint has to be rabbeted by hand, using a sharp chisel.

Fortunately, the dovetails don't need to be cut by hand. With a router, a dovetail bit and a dovetail jig, you can produce these traditional joints quickly and accurately. My dovetail jig is designed to be used with a 3/8-in. dovetail bit. A bushing around the shank of the bit rides against the fingers on the jig. The jig enables you to clamp the joining pieces at a right angle to each other and mill both sides of the joint at once. I set up the stock and mill first one corner, then the other (photo 6-4). After chiseling out the top part of the joint, I test the fit. Photo 6-5 shows how the extension's sides and front fit together.

As soon as the 3-piece extension is glued together, it can be glued in turn to the vanity's sides and top frame. Use a pipe clamp along each side, and one across the front (photo 6-6). For extra holding power, drive $1^1/4$-in. drywall screws down through the top frame and into the rabbet in each side extension piece.

6-4 Use the dovetail jig to cut the dovetailed corners in the cabinet extension pieces.

6-5 This test-fit shows how a side extension piece joins the front extension piece. The top $1^3/8$ in. of the joint is rabbeted, instead of dovetailed. Trim the joint by hand, if necessary, before gluing the parts together.

6-6 After the 3-piece extension assembly has been glued together, it can be glued in turn to the top frame and to the front edges of the sides. Clamp the cabinet along its length and width, as shown.

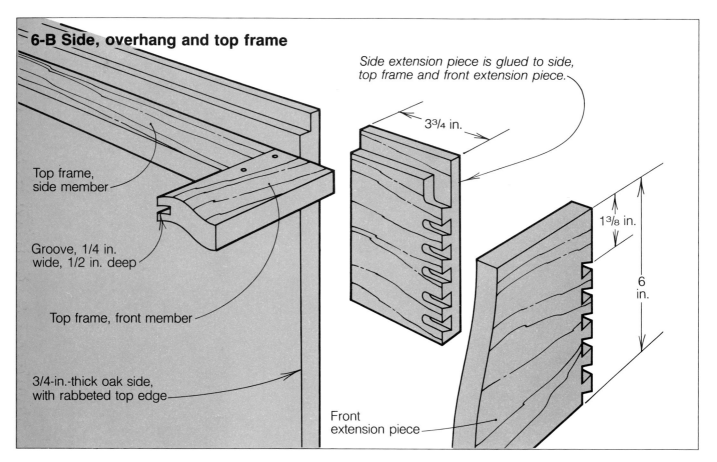

6-B Side, overhang and top frame

Side extension piece is glued to side, top frame and front extension piece.

3³/₄ in.

Top frame, side member

Groove, 1/4 in. wide, 1/2 in. deep

Top frame, front member

3/4-in.-thick oak side, with rabbeted top edge

Front extension piece

1³/₈ in.

6 in.

6-7 The first step in mortising a hinge is to screw the hinge in place and scribe around it with a sharp utility knife.

Face frame and base

Made from 1³/₄-in.-wide oak, the face frame covers the front edge of the bottom shelf and also the front edges of the sides. This frame is fairly easy to build. There are only 2 stiles, or vertical members, and 2 rails. I use lap joints where stiles and rails meet at the corners. The stiles are 23¹/₄ in. long, and they lap over the 36-in.-long rails.

I mill the lap joints using the radial arm saw and dado head, making several passes to complete each lap. The dado cutter should be adjusted to its maximum width, and depth of cut should be 3/8 in., or half the thickness of the face frame stock.

Before gluing the face frame together, I take time out to mortise the door hinges in the stiles. Each door swings on a pair of brass butt hinges with 3/4-in.-wide leaves, and it's easier to mortise the hinges before the face frame is joined together and installed.

The hinges I use have very thin leaves, so it's only necessary to mortise them into the stiles. The first step is to actually screw the hinges in place on the stiles after pre-drilling the holes. I position each hinge 2 in. away from the lap joint that marks the corner of the face frame. When the hinges are screwed fast, I scribe their locations into the stiles using a sharp utility knife (photo 6-7). Then I remove the hinges and deepen the scribed borders of each mortise. Working inside the scribed lines, I use hammer and chisel to make a series of parallel cuts across the grain. These cuts should be only as deep as the

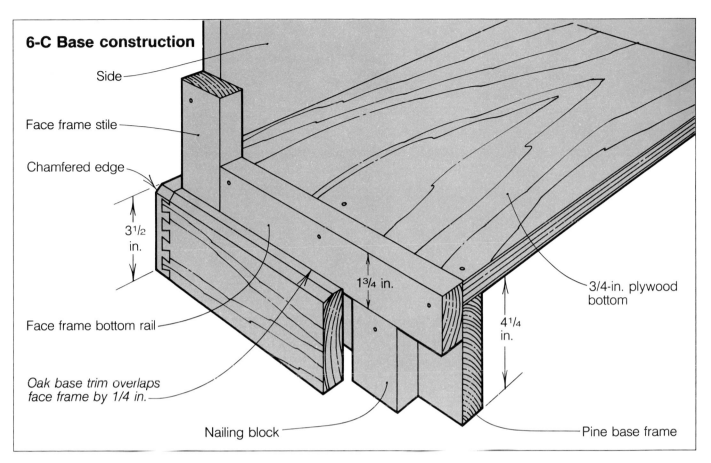

6-C Base construction

Side

Face frame stile

Chamfered edge

$3^1/2$ in.

Face frame bottom rail

Oak base trim overlaps
face frame by 1/4 in.

$1^3/4$ in.

3/4-in. plywood
bottom

$4^1/4$ in.

Nailing block

Pine base frame

thickness of the hinge leaf. Finally, use the chisel to pare out the waste inside the scribed lines (photo 6-8).

With the hinge mortises cut, the face frame can be assembled and installed. After spreading glue on the lap joints, I screw them together, driving #6 flat-head, 1/2-in. screws from the back of each joint. I use 2 screws per joint, pre-drilling and coutersinking the screws. As soon as it's together, the face frame can be attached to the carcase with glue and 6d finish nails. To avoid bending nails and splitting the oak, it's a good idea to pre-drill your nail holes. Use a bit that's just a tad smaller than the gauge of your nails.

Like the overhang near the top of the vanity, the base trim consists of 3 oak pieces that join with dovetailed corners. The front trim piece is $36^3/4$ in. long and $3^1/2$ in. wide. Side pieces are $19^3/4$ in. long and $3^1/2$ in. wide. I set these pieces up in the dovetail jig and mill the joints just as I did before. After gluing the base together, I nail it to the sides and front of the vanity. Along the front of the vanity, 3/4-in.-thick nailing blocks need to be installed beneath the face frame to provide solid backing for the base trim. I use a nailing block at each corner, plus one near the middle. As shown in drawing 6-C, the top edge of the base trim should overlap the bottom edge of the face frame by 1/4 in. To finish off the base, I set all the finishing nails and sand the trim on all three sides. Then I chuck a chamfering bit in the router and chamfer the top edge of the base trim, as shown in the drawing.

6-8 Unscrew the hinge and make a series of parallel cuts across the width of the mortise, then pare out the waste.

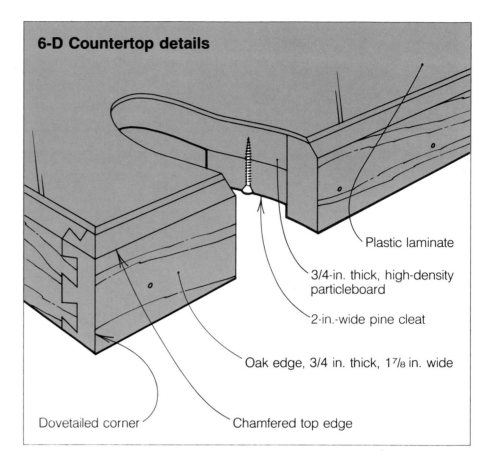

6-D Countertop details

Plastic laminate

3/4-in. thick, high-density particleboard

2-in.-wide pine cleat

Oak edge, 3/4 in. thick, 1⅞ in. wide

Dovetailed corner

Chamfered top edge

6-9 *For best results when laminating, both surfaces to be joined must be smooth. I use a belt sander to smooth the oak trim pieces flush with the particleboard surface.*

6-10 *With a scrap piece of laminate, I spread contact cement evenly over the underside of the plastic laminate. Give the particleboard and oak trim the same treatment.*

The laminate top

Construction details for the top of the vanity are shown in drawing 6-D. To make the top, you'll need to start with 3/4-in.-thick, high-density particleboard. Particleboard makes a good substrate for plastic laminate because it's very smooth, dense and stable, as long as it stays dry. Use a good carbide-tipped blade in your circular saw or table saw to cut the particleboard to its finished dimensions: 36½ in. by 22¼ in.

Now glue and screw 2-in.-wide pine cleats to the underside of the particleboard around all 4 edges. Use 1¼-in. drywall screws to make sure that screw points don't protrude through the top of the particleboard.

I give the vanity top an oak edge along its sides and front. The edge strips are 3/4 in. thick and 1⅞ in. wide. After cutting all 3 pieces to their finished lengths (23 in. for the sides; 37¼ in. for the front), I dovetail the corners, again using the dovetail jig. Then I glue front and side pieces together and attach the trim to the top with glue and 4d finish nails. The top edge of the oak trim should be flush with the top face of the particleboard.

Gluing the laminate to the top is the next step. One of the secrets behind a good laminating job is a substrate that's perfectly smooth. The slightest irregularity in the surface can create an air bubble and prevent the contact cement from bonding laminate to substrate. With this in mind, I place the top on the vanity and go over its surface thoroughly with the belt sander, using a medium-grit sanding belt (photo 6-9). Pay particular attention to the edges where particleboard and oak trim meet. When you're satisfied that the surface is smooth, brush or vacuum it free of dust.

I chose white plastic laminate for the top of this vanity, but you might want another color, depending on your taste and the setting where the vanity will be installed. There are dozens of laminate colors and finishes to choose from. I cut the laminate sheet a couple of inches oversize on the table saw, then place it upside-down on my workbench.

Contact cement can be messy stuff, but with a little care, it's not difficult to use. Before you start to work with it, make sure that you have adequate ventilation. The contact cement that I use is flammable, and produces vapors that can be hazardous to breathe. So I follow the safety precautions printed on the can, giving the workshop plenty of ventilation.

Instead of applying a single heavy layer of contact cement, I like to apply 2 thin layers to both surfaces that will be joined. There are special trowels for spreading contact cement, but I often use a scrap piece of laminate (photo 6-10). Aim for even coverage, especially around the edges. It's important to smooth out any bubbles or gobs of adhesive.

Depending on the temperature in your workshop, it will take 10-20 minutes for the adhesive to dry. When you can touch it with your finger without pulling away any adhesive, it's time to join the materials

6-11 With thin wood strips positioned across the top, align the laminate and then pull out one strip at a time. Remove the center strips first and force the laminate down firmly against the top.

6-12 To trim the laminate flush, I use a router and a carbide-tipped, flush-trim bit with a pilot bearing. Go around all 4 sides of the top.

6-13 With a chamfering bit in the router, I give the sides and front of the countertop their finished edge treatment.

together. Place 4 narrow strips of wood across the top, and then place the laminate on top of these strips (photo 6-11). Align the laminate so that it overlaps the top on all 4 sides. Then carefully remove first one center strip, then the other. Press the laminate firmly against the top. When you're sure the center section of laminate is flat and firmly adhered, remove the outer wood strips one at a time. Use a roller or a piece of wood to press the laminate firmly against the top.

Trimming is the next step. For this you'll need the router and a flush-trimming bit designed for plastic laminate. The bit I use has a bearing located under carbide cutters. Both the bearing and the cutters have the same diameter. I adjust the bit's depth so that the bearing rides against the top's oak edge while the cutters trim the laminate flush with the oak (photo 6-12).

A perfectly square countertop corner doesn't wear well or look good. There are a number of different edge treatments for laminate tops. The chamfered edge that I use on this vanity is one of my favorites. Using a chamfering bit with a pilot bearing in the router, I mill a delicate chamfer that extends across both the laminate's thickness and the oak trim (photo 6-13).

Door construction

The vanity has traditional frame-and-panel doors. The frames consist of vertical stiles and horizontal rails. Inside each door frame, a raised panel fits in grooves milled in stiles and rails. For this project, I decided to install the raised sides of the panels so that they face inside, but you might prefer to have them face outside.

It's best to build the door frames first, then cut the panel stock to size and "raise" the panels. I make the stiles and rails for this vanity 2 in. wide. At the corners of the frames, tenons in the rails fit into mortises in the stiles. Because the tenons extend all the way through the stiles, they're called "through" tenons. These tenons also have "haunches," or offsets, which fit into the panel grooves at the ends of the stiles (see drawing 6-E).

The dimensions of the face frame opening determine the sizes of stiles, rails and panels. The door opening in my vanity measures 19¼ in. high by 32 in. wide. Doors should be sized so that there's about 1/16 in. of clearance around all 4 sides of each door. I cut my stiles 19⅛ in. long and my rails 15⅞ in. long. Remember that the rail's length has to include a pair of 2-in.-long tenons.

Before mortises and tenons can be cut, the inside edges of stiles and rails need to be grooved to accept the panel. I set up the dado head in the table saw for this operation. The dado's width should be 3/8 in., and the cutter should be raised 3/8 in. above the table. Adjust the rip fence so that the groove will be centered exactly along the edge of your stock. Since my pieces are 3/4 in. thick, I set the fence 3/16 in. from the cutter.

When all the grooves are milled, I cut the mortises in the stiles, using a 3/8-in. hollow-chisel mortiser set up in the drill press. This special mortising accessory enables me to cut square-edged mortises very quickly and accurately (photo 6-14). If you don't have one, use a 3/8-in.

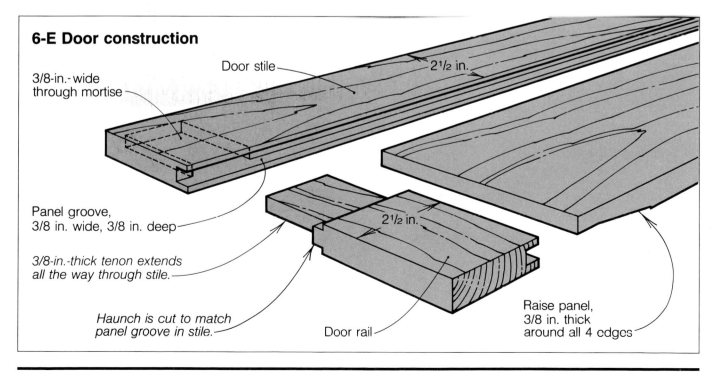

6-E Door construction

3/8-in.-wide through mortise

Door stile — 2½ in.

Panel groove, 3/8 in. wide, 3/8 in. deep

3/8-in.-thick tenon extends all the way through stile.

Haunch is cut to match panel groove in stile.

Door rail

2½ in.

Raise panel, 3/8 in. thick around all 4 edges

6-14 Mortises in the stiles of the door frames are milled on the drill press, using a 3/8-in.-wide hollow-chisel mortiser. Hold the stile firmly against a wood fence and make a series of plunge-cuts to complete each mortise.

Forstner bit to drill out the mortises; then chisel the edges square by hand.

I cut all the rail tenons on the table saw, using the dado head. The shoulders and cheeks of the tenons are cut first, with the dado adjusted for maximum width and raised 3/16 in. above the table. A wood gauge block, clamped to the rip fence on your side of the table, is positioned to align the rail for its shoulder cut. Holding each rail against the miter gauge, I make repeated passes through the cutter to remove the waste around each tenon's cheeks and shoulders (photo 6-15). To cut the haunches, I raise the cutter 1/2 in. above the table, and move the gauge block so that it's 3/8 in. closer to the cutter. Hold the rails on edge against the miter gauge to cut out the haunches (photo 6-16).

When you've finished all stiles and rails for the doors, it's a good idea to test-fit the frames together, making sure that tenons and mortises mate well. You can also take the inside measurements of the frames and figure out what size to make the panels. If the panel groove inside the frame is 3/8 in. deep, then you can get panel dimensions by adding 5/8 in. to the inside dimensions of the door frame. This formula allows 1/16 in. of expansion space around panel edges.

After cutting the panels to size, I "raise" the edges on the radial arm saw, using a molding head equipped with panel cutters. Because of the amount of wood being removed and the hardness of the oak, each edge has to be raised in stages. I adjust the radial arm saw to progressively lower settings, until the thickness at the outer edges of the panels is 3/8 in. (photo 6-17)

6-15 A wood gauge block, clamped to the rip fence, is positioned to align each rail for its shoulder cut. After making the shoulder cut, make repeated passes with the rail held against the miter gauge to complete each tenon cheek.

6-16 To cut the haunch in each tenon, move the gauge block 3/8 in. closer to the cutter and raise the cutter 1/2 in. above the table. Hold the rail on edge against the miter gauge as you move the tenon through the cutter.

6-17 After cutting the 3/4-in.-thick oak panels to size, I raise the edges on the radial arm saw, using a molding head and panel cutters. Mill the edges in stages, lowering the cutters until edge thickness is 3/8 in.

Now the doors can be assembled. Only the mortises and tenons are glued together. The panel "floats" in its frame, so that it can expand and contract without affecting frame size or stability. My approach when assembling traditional doors like these is to glue 3 sides of the frame together first. Then I slide the panel into its groove and glue the final frame member in place (photo 6-18). After wiping away any glue squeeze-out from around the joints, I clamp the frame together until the glue sets.

Finishing up

You'll probably want a backsplash along the back edge of the vanity, especially if you plan to install a sink. My backsplash is 3/4 in. thick and 4 in. high. For a better appearance, I chamfer the top and side edges of the backsplash before screwing it to the countertop from underneath with 2¹/₂-in. drywall screws (photo 6-19).

To show off the grain of the oak and the joinery details, I gave my vanity a clear finish: a coat of sanding sealer followed by 2 coats of satin urethane. The sanding sealer should be applied both inside and outside the cabinet as a precaution against moisture damage. For the same reason, I detached the backsplash from the countertop and finished it separately, making sure to apply urethane to both sides and all edges. When the finish dried, I bedded the bottom edge of the backsplash in a bead of silicone caulk when screwing it back on the countertop. The caulk should prevent water from seeping under the oak backsplash and damaging it.

6-18 Slide the panel into its groove after assembling 3 sides of the frame; then glue the final stile in place.

6-19 The backsplash is 4 in. high, with side and top edges chamfered. Attach it by screwing up through the back of the countertop.

Chapter 7

Trestle table

T he trestle table is a widely used design, and you'll find many versions and vintages in homes, antique shops and furniture stores. The best trestle tables seem to convey both strength and grace at the same time. This particular design is based on an old table I discovered on Nantucket, in one of the island's oldest homes.

Like many old tables, this one is built with mortise-and-tenon joints. Four wood pins and a pair of tusk tenons hold the table and its trestle base together. The tusk tenon is one of the earliest "take-apart" joints. Properly made, it can be as strong as it is easy to disassemble. In about a minute, the table can be broken down into easily moveable parts. This take-apart feature made the trestle table ideal for the small Colonial home, where a single room had to serve several purposes. Today this appeal still holds. From a craftsman's point of view, the opportunity to work with fine hardwood and make tusk tenon joints presents quite an enjoyable challenge.

In search of stock

To make this table, I started out with cherry boards that were about 1⁵/₈ in. thick. Most lumber yards refer to this material as "six quarter," or "6/4" stock. I bought my boards roughsawn, still showing the coarse, uneven surfaces of lumber that hasn't been planed smooth.

Lumber yards generally have a limited selection of hardwood in stock, so you may have to special-order your wood, or deal directly with a sawmill. Regardless of where you get your wood, make sure it's dry. Roughsawn stock, especially if it comes straight from the sawmill, usually contains more moisture than it should for fine furniture work. Technically, the wood you use should have a moisture content below 14%. If the wood has too much moisture, it may warp and shrink after you've finished the table, leaving you with irregular surfaces and ill-fitting joints to contend with. To make sure I'd be working with uniformly dry stock, I ordered my cherry "KD," which is short for kiln-dried. KD wood costs a little more, but it eliminates your moisture worries.

I used a thickness planer to take my roughsawn boards down to their finished thickness of 1³/₈ in. The planer I use is a portable model, quite a bit less expensive than the large stationary planers you'll find in commercial cabinet shops. With a planer like this, you can transform roughsawn wood into smooth lumber, or take stock that's too thick for your project down to a thinner dimension. If you don't have a planer, a woodworking friend with one could help you prepare your wood. Otherwise, you can pay a cabinet shop or lumber yard to plane your boards.

All the boards used to make this table should be 1³/₈ in. thick. Make sure to plane all the wood you'll need at the beginning of the project. It's frustrating if you have to stop in the middle of the job to plane an extra board. With my planer, I removed a maximum of about 1/16 in. with each pass. By running each board through progressively narrower settings and alternating the sides being planed, I eventually reached a finished thickness of 1³/₈ in. (photo 7-1).

Though the faces of the boards were smooth, board edges were still fairly uneven. I used the table saw and jointer to square up the stock. Before jointing an edge smooth and square, I ripped it as straight as possible on the table saw. Once a board has one true edge, it's easy to rip the opposite edge straight and square by setting up the rip fence on the table saw.

Look through your boards and choose the best ones for the top of the table. Before trimming to final size, the top should be at least 32 in. wide and 88 in. long. Shift the top boards around, orienting them so that the grain patterns are pleasing to the eye. For strength and stability, the growth rings in adjacent boards should show an alternating pattern: bark side up, bark side down. When you're satisfied with the combination and orientation of the boards, glue and clamp them up. Use wood pads between the metal clamping feet and the cherry, and tighten the bar clamps gradually to exert even pressure. A top this size needs at least 4 clamps.

Curved feet

Each trestle foot is made from 2 pieces of cherry. Each piece starts out 28 in. long, 3¹/₂ in. wide, and 1³/₈ in. thick. Before the curves are cut to give the feet their graceful shape, the pieces must be dadoed and then glued together. When assembled in pairs, the dadoes face each other, creating a "through" mortise that's 1 in. wide and 8 in. long. As shown in drawing 7-B, each leg piece requires a dado 1/2 in. deep and 8 in. wide. I mill these dadoes on the radial arm saw by making multiple passes with a dado head. Adjust the dado for maximum width of cut and 1/2-in. depth of cut. Working inside the layout lines, draw

7-1 I use a thickness planer to transform roughsawn cherry boards into smooth, uniformly thick stock.

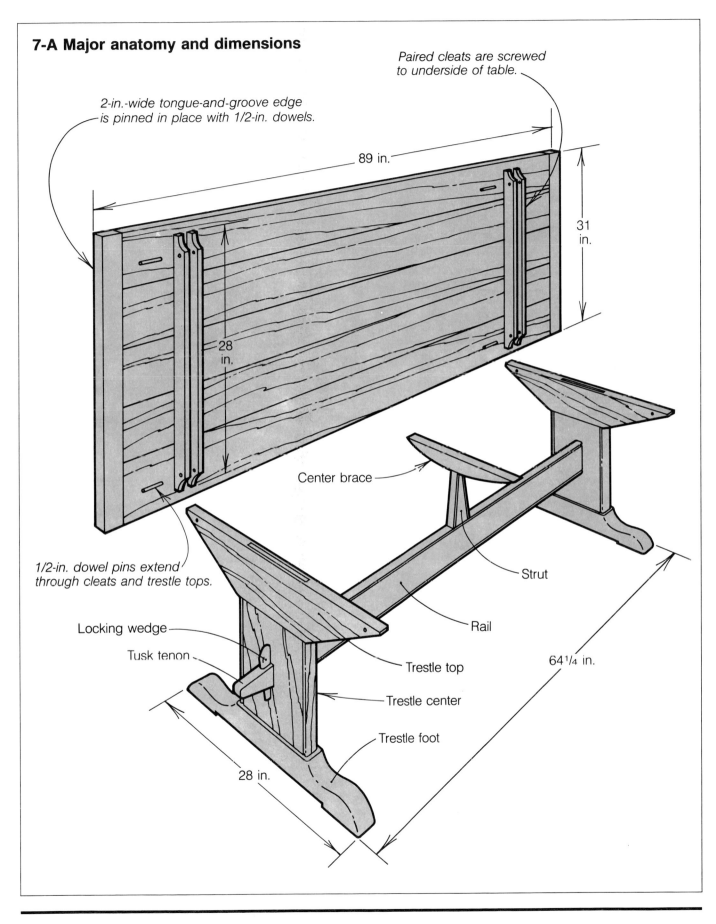

7-A Major anatomy and dimensions

Paired cleats are screwed to underside of table.

2-in.-wide tongue-and-groove edge is pinned in place with 1/2-in. dowels.

89 in.

31 in.

28 in.

Center brace

1/2-in. dowel pins extend through cleats and trestle tops.

Strut

Rail

64¼ in.

Locking wedge

Tusk tenon

Trestle top

Trestle center

Trestle foot

28 in.

the cutter through the stock with slow, steady pressure (photo 7-2). When all the joints are cut, smooth out any irregularities with a chisel or sanding block. Then glue and clamp each pair of foot pieces together.

After the glue has set, you can unclamp the leg stock in order to trace and cut the curves. The curve I use is basically an extended "ogee" shape that starts at the outside edge of the leg and ends 6 in. from the center. To get the same curve in each leg piece, I use a template made from a scrap piece of wood (photo 7-3). The leg profile includes a small "heel" at the outer edges of each foot. About 3/8 in. thick and 4 in. long, this heel gives the trestle added stability, especially over carpeted or uneven floors.

To saw curves in 2³/4-in.-thick cherry, you'll need a good bandsaw and a sharp, 1/4-in. blade. Double check the bandsaw table to make sure it's square with the blade, and feed the stock with slow, steady pressure (photo 7-4). After cutting the curves, saw out the heels too. While I'm at the bandsaw, I also cut out the curves in the 4 cleats that will be fastened to the underside of the table. These cleats, 28 in. long and 2¹/2 in. wide, are screwed to the table in pairs, and fit on either side of the trestle tops. As with the trestle feet, I use a template to trace the short curve in the end of each cleat.

I go over the top edges of the feet with a 3/8-in. roundover bit chucked in my router. This is also a good time to do some general smoothing of the feet and cleats. I use a drum sander (fitted with medium-grit paper) chucked in a drill press to remove any saw marks or unevenness in the feet and cleats (photo 7-5). If you don't have a drill press, a portable drill and drum sander attachment will also work.

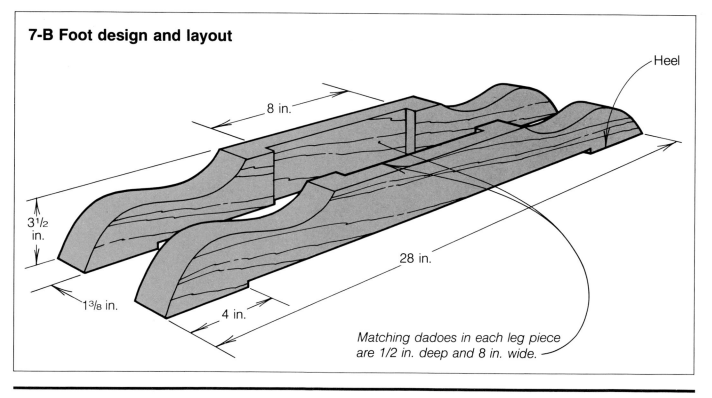

7-B Foot design and layout

Heel

8 in.

3¹/2 in.

1³/8 in.

4 in.

28 in.

Matching dadoes in each leg piece are 1/2 in. deep and 8 in. wide.

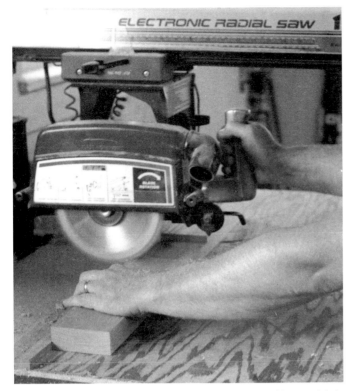

7-2 *Mill the broad dado in each foot piece by making multiple passes with the dado head. Adjust the cutter for maximum width of cut. Depth of cut should be 1/2 in.*

7-3 *I use a template made from a scrap piece of wood to trace the curve in each foot.*

7-4 *Cut out the curved feet on the bandsaw. To cut curves in hardwood this thick, you'll need a sharp, 1/4-in. blade.*

7-5 *A drum sander, chucked in a drill press, does a good job of removing saw marks and irregularities after curved cuts are made.*

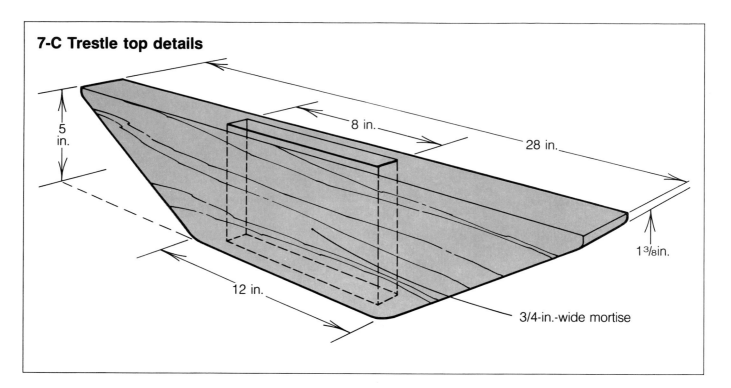

7-C Trestle top details

5 in.

8 in.

28 in.

1³⁄₈ in.

12 in.

3/4-in.-wide mortise

Making the trestle top

Each trestle top is 1³⁄₈ in. thick, 5 in. wide and 28 in. long. A pair of angled cuts give each top a tapered profile, and a mortise holds the tenoned center piece of the trestle (see drawing 7-C). The mortise in the top is 3/4 in. wide and 8 in. long. It extends all the way through the top.

I drilled out the mortises in the trestle tops and then chiseled them square. You have to drill and chisel from both sides of the mortise. After laying out the rectangular opening on one edge of the stock, use a square to transfer the mortise outline to the opposite edge.

The best way to drill out mortises is with a drill press and a Forstner bit. The drill press ensures that the holes will be vertical, which is important. The Forstner bit is ideal for mortising because it doesn't wander, even when overlapping holes are being drilled. Use a fence and featherboard set-up to brace the stock on the drill press table (see photo 7-6). Position the fence so that the 3/4-in. bit is centered exactly between the layout lines. Then clamp the featherboard to the table so that it forces the stock tightly against the fence. Working inside the layout lines, make a row of overlapping holes, drilling to a depth of just over 2¹⁄₂ in. Then flip the stock and drill in from the opposite edge. To finish the mortise, chisel all the edges square, working from both sides of the joint (photo 7-7).

To complete the trestle tops, you need to make the angled cuts to create a tapered profile. As shown in drawing 7-C, the taper begins 3/8 in. down from the top edge of the piece and ends 6 in. from the center. The angle is about 60 degrees. After marking your layout lines on the stock, adjust your table saw's miter gauge to match the angle,

7-6 Use a 3/4-in. Forstner bit to drill out the mortise in each trestle top. A featherboard, clamped to the drill press table, keeps the stock braced firmly against the fence.

7-7 With a sharp chisel, square up the edges of the mortises and smooth the inside of the joint.

7-8 I reverse the miter gauge in its guide slot on the table saw to make the angled cuts in the trestle tops.

and use the gauge to guide the stock through the blade. You'll notice that in photo 7-8, I make these angled cuts by reversing the miter gauge in its guide slot and pushing the stock through the blade behind the gauge. This switch gives me a little more control over the cut. After the angle cuts are made, go over them with the drum sander. I take a few extra minutes on the drum sander to round over the corners at the top of each angled cut.

Tenons and mortises in the center pieces

The center piece of each trestle is tenoned on both ends and has a mortise in its middle. The center's width is 10 in.; its thickness, 1³/₈ in. The overall length (including tenons) is 27¹/₄ in., with 19¹/₈ in. between tenons (see drawing 7-D). This puts your table top 29 in. above the floor, which is a comfortable height for most people. If you want your table higher or lower, simply make the center pieces longer or shorter.

The tenons on this piece are fairly large, and I mill them using the radial arm saw and dado cutter. Adjust the cutter to its maximum width. Depth of cut for the 3/4-in.-thick top tenon will be 5/16 in. To cut the 1-in.-thick bottom tenon, depth of cut should be 3/16 in. Don't just rely on these figures when setting up. Mill sample tenons in scrap stock that's exactly the same thickness as your center piece. Test-fit these tenons in the mortises you've already made in top and leg pieces. When you get a snug fit, the dado's depth of cut is right, and you can mill the tenons by making repeated passes with the cutter.

The next step is to trim 1 in. from the sides of each tenon so that

7-D Trestle center joinery

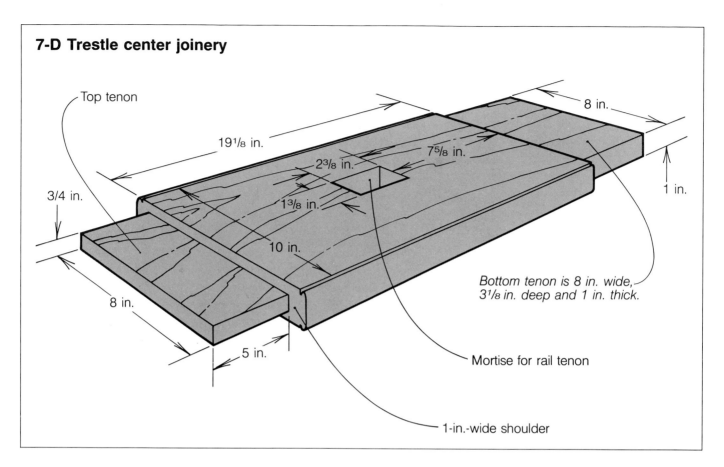

Top tenon

19¹⁄₈ in.

8 in.

2³⁄₈ in.

7⁵⁄₈ in.

3/4 in.

1³⁄₈ in.

1 in.

10 in.

8 in.

5 in.

Bottom tenon is 8 in. wide, 3¹⁄₈ in. deep and 1 in. thick.

Mortise for rail tenon

1-in.-wide shoulder

7-9 *Use a back saw to trim the tenon sides in the trestle center piece.*

7-10 *With an orbital sander and medium-grit paper, I smooth out the tenon cheeks and sides to get a better fit in the mortise.*

7-11 *After drilling out the mortise in each trestle center piece, chisel it square from both sides.*

they can fit into their 8-in.-long mortises. I do this trimming by hand, using a back saw (photo 7-9). Finish the tenons up by smoothing the "cheeks," or broad tenon faces, with some medium-grit sandpaper. You can do this sanding by hand, or use an orbital sander, as shown in photo 7-10.

The trestle center pieces aren't complete until you've cut mortises for the stretcher, or rail, that connects both trestles. Measurements for laying out this pair of mortises are shown in drawing 7-D. These mortises have to be drilled out and then chiseled square, just like the mortises in the trestle tops. Bore a series of overlapping holes inside the layout lines for each mortise, this time drilling all the way through the stock. To avoid chipping out where the drill leaves the cherry, place some scrap wood underneath the joint. Square up the edges and inside surfaces of the mortise with a sharp chisel (photo 7-11).

A pair of tusk tenons

It isn't difficult to understand where this joint gets its name once you've had a look at a completed one. The tapered wedge that holds the tenon fast in its mortise looks a bit like a tusk protruding on either side of a wooden snout. Tapping down on the wider upper edge of the wedge effectively tightens the joint, while tapping up allows you to remove the wedge and pull the tenon free.

The tusk tenon joint is a tricky one to make. Be sure to take plenty of time laying out the different tapered cuts that have to be made in the tenon and the mortise (see drawing 7-E). The first step, of course, is to dimension the rail. This one is $5^{1}/_{2}$ in. wide, $1^{3}/_{8}$ in. thick, and $71^{1}/_{2}$ in. long, including a pair of $7^{3}/_{8}$-in.-long tenons.

The shoulder-to-shoulder distance between rail tenons is $64^{1}/_{4}$ in. Each tenon starts out $1^{3}/_{8}$ in. wide and $2^{3}/_{8}$ in. high (the same dimensions as the mortises in the trestle centers). At $1^{5}/_{8}$ in. from the shoulder, the tenon starts to taper down to a finished height of $1^{7}/_{8}$ in. (tenon width stays the same). The taper is a traditional tusk tenon detail, and makes it easier to fit the long tenon in its mortise. After carefully laying out these joints on the rail, I cut them out on the bandsaw.

The next step is to mill the mortise for the wedge. I drilled these mortises out on the drill press, using a 1/2-in. Forstner bit. The 1/2-in.-wide mortise is centered in the rail tenon and begins $1^{1}/_{4}$ in. from the rail tenon's shoulder. This end of the mortise is cut straight down through the rail tenon. The opposite end of the mortise tapers inward 5 degrees, matching the taper of the wedge. The mortise opening that faces up should be $1^{3}/_{4}$ in. long; the opening that faces down should measure $1^{3}/_{8}$ in. long.

To cut the tapered end of the mortise, I use a tapered shim, positioned under the rail. If the shim is tapered 5 degrees, the end of the mortise will have the same taper (see photo 7-12). Unlike most mortises, these don't have to be squared up, but you'll still have to

7-E Tusk tenon details

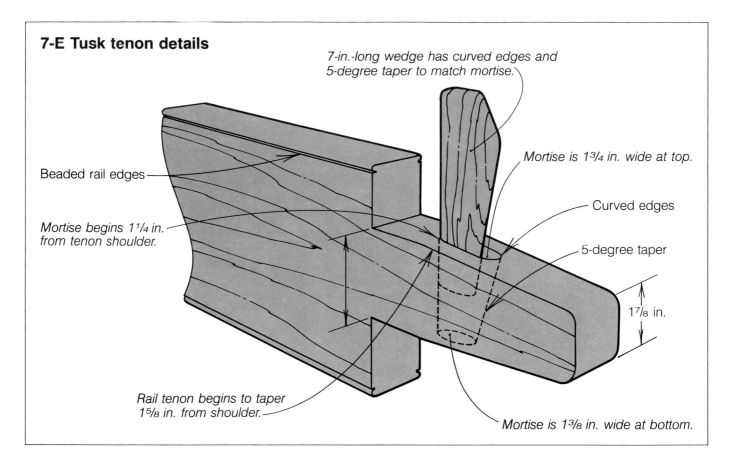

7-in.-long wedge has curved edges and 5-degree taper to match mortise.

Beaded rail edges

Mortise is 1³/₄ in. wide at top.

Curved edges

Mortise begins 1¹/₄ in. from tenon shoulder.

5-degree taper

1⁷/₈ in.

Rail tenon begins to taper 1⁵/₈ in. from shoulder.

Mortise is 1³/₈ in. wide at bottom.

7-12 *By positioning a 5-degree wedge underneath the rail on the drill press table, you can drill out the tapered mortise for the tusk tenon. Use a 1/2-in. Forstner bit.*

7-13 *I use a molding head with beading cutters to mill a bead along all 4 edges of the rail. On this table saw set-up, the stock is held against a wood auxiliary fence and run through a single bead cutter.*

smooth the sides of each mortise with a chisel. Once this is done, you can cut out the tapered wedges. Spend some time smoothing these small but important pieces after they're cut. I use medium-grit sandpaper to ease the edges, then go over each wedge thoroughly with fine-grit paper.

The center support should be made next. It consists of a tapered vertical strut and a curved horizontal brace. The strut tapers from a width of 2³/₈ in. where it joins the rail to a width of 1³/₈ in. where it joins the brace. Both ends of the strut have tenons, and these should be cut before the tapering cuts are made along the strut sides. The lower tenon is 3/4 in. thick and 1³/₈ in. wide. It extends 1 in. into a mortise cut in the rail. The strut's upper tenon, measuring 3/4 in. square, extends all the way through the brace.

Tables like this one often received some sort of edge treatment. With this in mind, I beaded the edges of the rail, the rail strut and trestle center pieces. To do this, I installed beading cutters, or "knives," in a molding head and fitted the head on my table saw. The molding head performs like a dado cutter, but can mill curves instead of dadoes. The beading cutters I have are designed to mill a row of 3 beads, but I only wanted to mill one. The solution was to "bury" 2 of the beads in a wood auxiliary fence that I clamped to the rip fence. I tested the set-up on some scrap stock before milling the edges of the trestle center pieces and the rail (photo 7-13).

Sanding is the last thing to do before gluing up the trestles and gluing the center brace to the rail. Start with a medium-grit paper to ease all corners and smooth any rough sections. Finish up with a fine-grit paper; then glue and clamp each trestle assembly together.

Topping off

The top has a 2-in.-wide breadboard edge along each end. This is a large-scale version of the edge detail used in chapter 5 on the bedside table. Covering the end grain of the boards used to make the top, the breadboard edge gives the table a more formal appearance and also helps to prevent warping. To join top to edge pieces, I used a tongue-and-groove joint, 3/4 in. wide and 1 in. deep.

Before milling the tongues and grooves, you have to cut each end of the top square. One good way to do this is to use a circular saw and a guide strip. By clamping a straight length of wood square with the table top's sides, you create a guiding edge for the base of your circular saw (photo 7-14). Use a good carbide-tipped blade, and position the straightedge so that the blade falls on the cut-off line.

The table top gets the tongue, and I mill it using a router, equipped with a fence and a 5/8-in. mortising bit. I adjust the fence so that the first pass will cut the shoulder of the tongue (photo 7-15). I also adjust the bit's depth so that after 2 passes are made on each side of the joint, a 3/4-in.-thick tongue remains. Use a hand saw to cut back the tongue at each corner of the table, since it's not supposed to extend

7-14 *You can trim the table top to its finished length using a circular saw and a straight length of wood. Clamped to the table top with its edge parallel to the cut-off line, the wood guides the base of the circular saw for a straight, square cut.*

through the ends of the breadboard edge.

The groove in each edge piece is milled on the table saw, using the dado head. I stop the groove about 3/4 in. short of the ends by lowering the edge piece over the cutter and then lifting it free before the cutter reaches the end. This technique is described in chapter 5. There is a significant difference here, however. Cherry is much harder to cut than pine, and the width of this groove is wider. For safety, it's important to use a dado cutter that's very sharp, and the full 1-in. depth of the groove should be cut in stages. For the first cut in each edge piece, raise the cutter just 1/2 in. or less above the table. Make successive cuts until you reach the finished depth of 1 in. Test your set-up and technique on some scrap cherry before you cut the edge grooves.

A table top with this width and thickness is bound to move as the wood gains or loses moisture in response to changing humidity conditions. Coats of varnish or other finish can reduce wood movement to some degree, but not eliminate it. Over time, a glued joint between the edge piece and the end grain of the top will fail because movement across the grain of the wood is usually greater than movement along the grain. So instead of gluing this joint, I pin it from underneath the table with 1/2-in. birch dowels. The dowels extend through the tongue and only partway into the wood on the upper side of the groove; they're not visible except from underneath the top.

7-15 To mill the tongue along the table's edge, use a router equipped with a fence and a straight bit. Two passes on either side of the joint should leave a tongue 3/4 in. thick and 1 in. deep. An edge strip, grooved using the dado head on the table saw, fits over this tongue.

I use 3 dowels in each tongue-and-groove joint: 1 at the center and 2 near the corners. Before drilling the dowel holes, the edge piece should be clamped firmly in place. The center dowel can be glued into its hole. But the corner holes in the tongues should be made into 3/4-in.-long slots that run parallel with the width of the table. The slots allow the table to expand and contract across its width without loosening the joint.

Sanding is the next step. Given the cost of the wood and the traditional joinery details, this table deserves a fine finish. Thorough sanding is crucial, especially on the top. I start with the belt sander, using a medium-grit sanding belt to remove major irregularities where the top's glued-up boards join, or where the edge pieces join the table. Switch to a fine-grit belt as the top becomes flat; then switch to an orbital pad sander and fine-grit paper. Go over the table completely until wood surfaces are uniformly smooth. An alternative to this painstaking work is to turn your table top over to a cabinet shop equipped with a stroke sander. With this large-scale sanding machine, you'll get a flat, smooth top that requires just a little touching up with fine-grit paper. You'll still have to go over the edges yourself.

Now round over the table's edges. I use a 1/2-in. roundover bit, chucked in a router, to radius all the corners and edges. Finally, attach the cleats to the underside of the table. I use 3 screws per cleat, and counterbore them with a 1/2-in. bit. The paired cleats should fit snugly over the trestle tops, and you may decide not to drill out the cleats and trestle tops and install 1/2-in. dowel pins to hold the trestle tops in place. These pins and their holes are shown in drawing 7-A.

This completes the table. With a fine wood like cherry, the finish you choose should show off the rich color of the wood but also protect it. In the old days, cabinetmakers would spend hours rubbing tung oil or linseed into the wood. This technique will still produce fine results, but if you want a less labor-intensive approach, try one of the newer penetrating oil finishes.

Chapter 8

Bookcase

Bookcase construction presented significant problems to early builders. Books were heavier in the days before paperbacks, and plywood wasn't available to add rigidity and racking resistance at the back of the bookcase. Almost always, bookcases and all kinds of shelves were built into a wall, backed up by structural framing or masonry.

Today, plywood and other wood-based sheet materials make it possible to build strong shelves that can stand on their own. Without sacrificing strength, a bookcase can be made light enough to take with you when you move house. Though the bookcase I've built here is moveable, I've added a few important details to give it a more formal, permanent presence. For example, the detailed head casing and base on this bookcase are traditional elements that you'll find on the built-in shelves in a fine library. And even though the sides and shelves of this bookcase are cut from plywood, there are no exposed plywood edges to give away the fact that this isn't solid wood.

This bookcase can be built as a single unit, or you can build several and gang them together to form a longer storage wall (see sidebar, pg. 115). Both the head casing and the base are removeable, so it's not difficult to convert a single unit into a double or triple unit. Keeping the shelf length at just under 3 ft. ensures that the shelves won't deflect under the fullest literary load.

Sides, top, bottom and back

Join these parts together and you've got the structural case. The sides, top, bottom and shelves are all cut from 3/4-in.-thick, birch-faced plywood. A sheet of 3/4-in.-thick plywood is difficult to handle alone, so don't attempt ripping a full sheet unless you've got a helper or at least a pedestal roller support to use with your table saw. As an alternative, you might be able to have these parts ripped to rough size at your lumber yard. Yards equipped with a panel cutter usually charge a small fee for cutting down plywood and other sheet materials. It's well worth it if you'll be transporting and handling the material alone.

The sides are 11 3/4 in. wide. The top is 11 1/2 in. wide. The bottom is 12 1/8 in. wide, and the shelves are 10 1/2 in. wide, not including the solid pine lip that will be fastened along the front edge of each shelf. After ripping sides, top, bottom, back and shelves to their finished widths, cut everything to final length. The sides are 77 3/8 in. long, the top is 36 in. long and the bottom is 35 1/4 in. long. Shelves are 34 3/8 in. long.

The joinery in this bookcase is fairly simple. The case is assembled with a combination of rabbet and dado joints that can be cut easily on the table saw, using a dado head. To get started, set up the dado head to cut 3/8 in. deep and 3/4 in. wide. Mill a sample dado to test for 3/8-in. depth and correct dado width. Sometimes, 3/4-in. plywood ends up being slightly thinner or thicker than it's supposed to be. Make sure to match your dado head's width of cut to the thickness of your stock. Aim for a fit that's snug but not forced. Once you're sure of the adjustment, the cutter can stay where it is for the next three milling operations. All you'll need to make are fence adjustments.

First, rabbet both ends of the top to fit over the top edges of the sides. Clamp an auxiliary wood fence (3/4 in. thick and about 3 in. high) in place so that the wood edge is even with the right edge of the dado cutter. To mill the rabbet, butt the top's end edge against the wood fence, and guide the top through the cutter with the miter gauge (see photo 8-1).

Next, dado the sides to receive the bottom of the case. The dado is milled 4 1/4 in. from the side's bottom edge. Move the auxiliary fence so that it's on your side of the blade. It should be located 4 1/4 in. from the inside, or nearest edge, of the dado cutter. Use the miter gauge to guide the side through the cutter for a right-angle cut (photo 8-2).

Now I rabbet the back edge of each side to hold the plywood back. Even though the back is just 1/4 in. thick, I like to set it in a 3/8-in.-deep rabbet to keep it out of sight. To mill these rabbets, I use the auxiliary fence in a different way. It's actually positioned partway over the dado cutter, so that only 3/8 in. of the cutter's 3/4-in. thickness shows (photo 8-3). If you haven't already done so, you can make a semicircular cutout in the wood fence by raising the dado cutter into the wood, stopping at 3/8-in. height. Run the back edge of the side against this set-up and mill a rabbet 3/8 in. wide and 3/8 in. deep.

8-A Major anatomy and dimensions

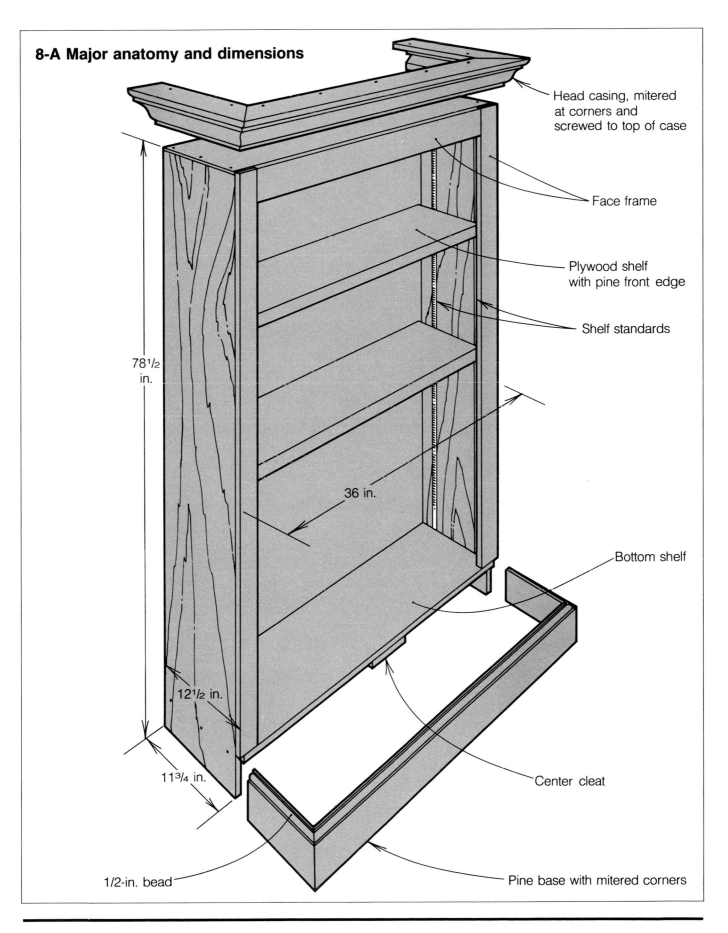

Head casing, mitered at corners and screwed to top of case

Face frame

Plywood shelf with pine front edge

Shelf standards

78 1/2 in.

36 in.

Bottom shelf

12 1/2 in.

Center cleat

11 3/4 in.

1/2-in. bead

Pine base with mitered corners

8-1 Set up the dado to cut 3/4 in. wide and 3/8 in. deep. To rabbet the top, position an wood auxiliary fence even with the right edge of the cutter. Using the miter gauge as a guide and the wood fence as a stop, run both ends of the top through the dado.

8-2 Dado the sides for the bottom shelf using the miter gauge. Position the auxiliary fence on your side of the cutter, and 4¼ in. to the right of it.

8-3 The sides have to be rabbeted to receive the back. Position the auxiliary fence partway over the cutter, so that only 3/8 in. of cutting width shows. Run the back edge of each side against the fence to mill the rabbet.

The next step is to dado the sides to receive the steel shelf standards. The standards have a shallow, U-shaped profile and they're meant to be used in sets of four: one pair on each side of the case. My standards require a dado 5/8 in. wide and 3/16 in. deep, but the ones you buy might be slightly different. Adjust the width and depth of the dado, testing it on scrap stock, until the fit is snug and flush. Then set the rip fence 1½ in. away from the cutter, and cut the dadoes closest to the front of the case. To mill the back pair of dadoes, set the fence 1⅞ in. away from the cutter. The extra 3/8 in. accounts for the 3/8-in.-deep rabbet at the back of the case (see drawing 8-B).

Now we're ready to assemble the case. I install the bottom first, using glue and 1⅝-in. drywall screws. As you snug the bottom into each side dado, make sure that the bottom's front edge extends 3/4 in. beyond the sides' front edges (photo 8-4). Combined with the base molding, the extra width of this bottom-most shelf gives the bookcase a stable, pleasing proportion, and also provides a wider shelf for oversize books.

Attach the top next. The top's dadoed ends fit over the sides, and the front edges of all three parts should be flush with each other. Glue both joints, and drive 1⅝-in. screws down into the sides to pull the joint tight.

Attaching the 1/4-in.-thick back effectively squares up the case. The back fits into the rabbeted sides, and should extend over the back edges of the bottom and top pieces (drawing 8-C). After spreading glue in the rabbets and along top and bottom edges, I first nail the back to the top of the case with 4d box nails. Then I compare diagonal measurements from opposite corners of the case. Sides, top

8-4 *The bottom shelf is glued and screwed into dadoed sides. Before driving screws, make sure that the bottom's front edge extends 3/4 in. beyond the sides' front edges.*

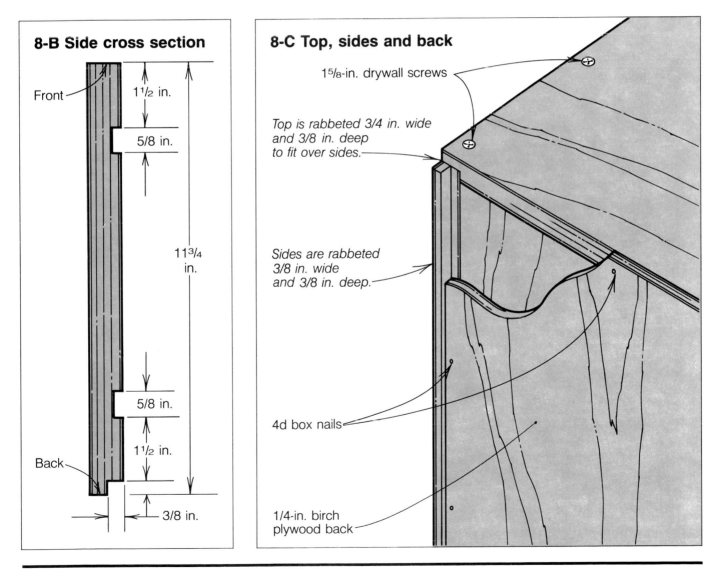

8-B Side cross section

Front

1½ in.

5/8 in.

11¾ in.

5/8 in.

1½ in.

Back

3/8 in.

8-C Top, sides and back

1⁵⁄₈-in. drywall screws

Top is rabbeted 3/4 in. wide and 3/8 in. deep to fit over sides.

Sides are rabbeted 3/8 in. wide and 3/8 in. deep.

4d box nails

1/4-in. birch plywood back

and bottom might have to be racked slightly until the diagonals match, which indicates that the case is square. Then I nail down the remaining 3 edges.

The face frame

A pair of side stiles and a top rail make up the face frame, which is fastened to the front of the case. The side stiles are 2 in. wide and 72³/4 in. long. The bottom end of each stile rests on the front corner of the bottom shelf, as shown in drawing 8-D. The top rail is 36 in. long and 4⁷/8 in. wide.

At the top corners of the face frame, stiles and the rail join with half-lap joints. I cut the half laps using a dado head on the radial arm saw. After setting the dado head for maximum width of cut, adjust the height of the saw so that the cutter removes exactly 3/8 in. of waste, or half the thickness of face frame members. You'll probably have to make test cuts and readjust the cutter's height until the depth of the lap joint is right.

On the side stiles, lap width is 4⁷/8 in., which is the width of the top rail. The rail's lap width is 2 in. Once you've marked these lap widths on the stock, you can cut the laps by making repeated passes with the dado cutter (photo 8-5). Test-fit the joints. If your dado head has left any surface irregularities that prevent a tight fit, smooth these out with a file or some medium-grit sandpaper. I glue the lap joints together pulling them tight with #8 5/8-in.-long screws. The screws are driven from the back of the rail, and their primary purpose is to keep the joint tight while the glue sets.

As soon as the face frame is together, you can fasten it to the case. Carefully spread glue over the plywood edges that will be covered (the front edges of the sides and top), and nail the frame in place with 6d finishing nails. To reduce the possibility of hammer marks marring the surface of the frame, I leave each nail head proud of the surface, then use a nail set to set the nail about 1/8 in. below the surface. I don't fill these holes until after stain or other finish has been applied. With finish on the wood, you can choose a wood putty or filler that matches the surrounding wood closely.

Building the base

The base wraps around the sides and front of the bookcase, its top edge covering the plywood edge of the bottom shelf. There are miter joints where the base sides meet the front, but before cutting these, I mill a decorative bead along the top edge of a single piece of pine that's 5 in. wide, 3/4 in. thick and at least 5¹/2 ft. long. A 1/2-in. beading bit, chucked in a router, gives the top edge of the base a pleasing profile (photo 8-6). After beading the edge, I cut the board into three pieces. Be sure to cut the base front and sides about 2 in. longer than their finished size to allow for mitering and trimming.

At 5 in., the base pieces are just a little too wide to miter with my

8-5 Lap joints in the face frame's stiles and rail can be cut on the radial arm saw, using a dado cutter. Set the dado for maximum width of cut and 3/8-in. depth of cut. Then make repeated passes to complete each joint.

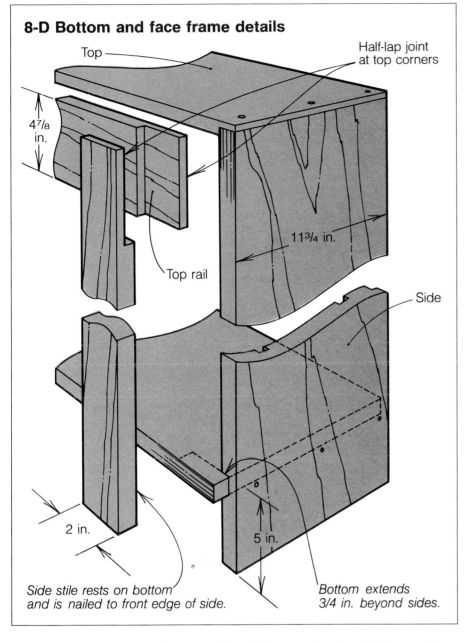

8-D Bottom and face frame details

Top

Half-lap joint
at top corners

$4^7/8$ in.

$11^3/4$ in.

Top rail

Side

2 in.

5 in.

Side stile rests on bottom
and is nailed to front edge of side.

Bottom extends
3/4 in. beyond sides.

chopsaw, so I cut the miters on the table saw. Set the blade to a 45-degree bevel, and test the angle of cut by running two scrap pieces through. If the resulting joint is square, you know the blade is beveled correctly. If not, readjust the bevel and test it again.

Before cutting miters, I make it a practice to pencil the orientation of the miter on each piece while holding it in place on the case. This way, I won't accidentally make the cut with the angle leaning in the wrong direction. When you cut the miters in the base sides, leave the square end of each piece long by at least 1/2 in. You can trim these ends square after getting a final tight fit at the miter joints. Miter the base front 1/32 in. longer than it needs to be. In other words, if your case is 36 in. wide, cut the miters $36^1/32$ in. apart from each other. This gives you an extra margin of safety when fitting the miter joints.

8-6 The base gets a decorative bead along its top edge, milled with a router and 1/2-in. beading bit. Use a clear piece of pine at least $5^1/2$ ft. long, so that you'll be able to cut sides and front out after milling a single edge.

Remember, it's better to have to trim a joint back than to come up short.

When the fit is right and the sides have been trimmed at their square ends, you can glue the base pieces together. I reinforce the miter joints with short blocks, glued and screwed in place along the back edge of each joint. If I'm building two or three bookcase units to be joined together, I don't glue the base or the head casing to the case (photo 8-7). This way, you can remove the trim, separate the units, and move them individually. Even with a single bookcase unit, it makes sense to detach the trim before moving the case.

Install the base by driving 1¼-in. drywall screws through the plywood sides and into the base sides. A short cleat, screwed to the bottom shelf, becomes a fastening point for the base front (drawing 8-E).

The head casing

Like the base, the head casing is designed to be detachable. Even if you're only building a single bookcase unit, it's wise to remove the head casing before moving the bookcase. This way, you can make sure the delicate trim won't be damaged in transit.

Though the casing may look complex, it isn't that difficult to build if you're able to cut good miter joints. The casing is made from three

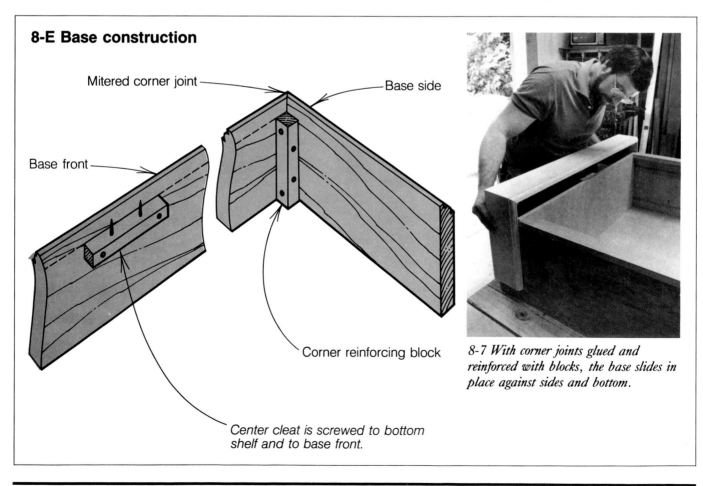

8-E Base construction

Mitered corner joint

Base side

Base front

Corner reinforcing block

Center cleat is screwed to bottom shelf and to base front.

8-7 With corner joints glued and reinforced with blocks, the base slides in place against sides and bottom.

different pieces of wood. The cap piece is 4½ in. wide and has a molded front edge. Then there's an angled cleat, and finally some common crown molding (see drawing 8-F). The molding I use here is 3⅝ in. wide. Crown molding comes in numerous widths and profiles, so you'll have to see what's available at your lumber yard. I chose this profile because it fits the scale of the bookcase nicely.

The first thing to do is to mill the curved front edge on the cap. Though there are 3 cap pieces, I mill the edge on a single long piece, and cut the miter joints afterwards. Select a clear, straight length (about 5½ ft.) of 3/4-in.-thick stock. The curve along the cap's top edge is cut using a router and a 1/4-in. roundover bit. To cut the curve along the cap's bottom edge, I switched to a 1/2-in. roundover bit. This slightly top-heavy profile looks nicer than one that's perfectly symmetrical.

Cut the miter joints in side and front cap pieces. When measuring for these miter cuts, remember that the cap should overhang the top by 2¾ in. on both the sides and the front of the case. Run the side pieces long at the back so that they can be trimmed after the corner joints are fit. I glue and screw the cap's miter joints together, using a jig to make screw pockets (see chapter 11, photo 11-9). Instead of using drywall screws, which tend to cause splitting in pocket holes, I drive #6 1½-in.-long pan-head screws to pull the joint tight. When the cap

8-8 *A wood stop block and an extra piece of angled cleat position the molding upside down in the power miter box while the miter is cut.*

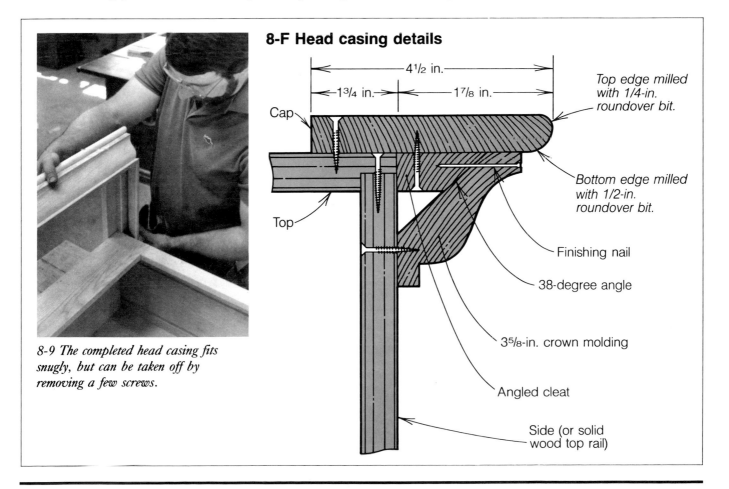

8-9 *The completed head casing fits snugly, but can be taken off by removing a few screws.*

8-F Head casing details

4½ in.

1¾ in.

1⅞ in.

Cap

Top

Top edge milled with 1/4-in. roundover bit.

Bottom edge milled with 1/2-in. roundover bit.

Finishing nail

38-degree angle

3⅝-in. crown molding

Angled cleat

Side (or solid wood top rail)

assembly is complete, screw it to the top of the case.

The next step is to cut the angled cleats and fasten them to the underside of the cap with glue and 1 1/4-in. drywall screws. As shown in drawing 8-F, the cleat is 1 7/8 in. wide (on its wider side) and one edge is ripped at a 38-degree angle. Miter the corner joints where side cleats meet the front cleat, but don't fuss in fitting these miters since they'll be hidden by the crown molding.

Now you're ready to miter and install the crown molding. You'll find that it's more difficult to get a clean, accurate miter in molded stock as opposed to square-edged stock. Whether you're using a powered "chopbox" or a hand saw and miter box, the molding has to be positioned carefully for cutting. As shown in photo 8-8, I clamp a wood fence to the base of my power miter box to orient the molding properly. This set-up braces the molding upside down, but at exactly the same angle it will have when installed.

Cut the front molding first, after carefully marking the location and direction of each miter cut. It's best to err on the long side when cutting this pair of miters. Miter the side pieces last, trimming the back edges square only after the miter joints fit tightly.

To install the crown molding, glue the miter joints together, and glue the top of the molding to the angled cleat and to the underside of the cap. Don't glue the bottom of the molding to the case, because then you won't be able to remove the head casing. I drive 4d finishing nails through the molding and into the cleat to pull the miter joints tight. While the completed head casing should fit snugly, you should also be able to pull it free after loosening a few screws, as shown in photo 8-9. If you need to tighten the fit where the bottom of the molding joins the case, you can drive screws into the molding from inside the case, as shown in drawing 8-F.

Shelves and standards

The front edges of the plywood shelves need to be covered with a solid pine lip. Apart from hiding the plywood edges, the solid wood stiffens the shelves and gives them better proportions. The lip is 3/4 in. thick and 1 5/8 in. wide. Using a 3/8-in. roundover bit on the router table, I round the front edges of the pine strips before attaching them with glue and 6d finishing nails (photo 8-10).

Install the shelving standards only after you've applied finish to the completed bookcase (photo 8-11). Depending on whether you finish your case with clear varnish, stain or paint, you can choose either plain steel standards or brass-plated ones. Sold along with the standards are snap-in shelf supports and short, ring-shanked installation nails. When nailing the standards in their dadoes, make sure you've got them right side up, and level with each other. This is easy to do if you refer to the letter or number guide marks stamped between slots or nail holes at regular intervals.

8-10 *The front edges of the plywood shelves are covered with solid wood edging 1⁵/₈ in. wide. After rounding over wood edging on the router table, glue and nail it to the shelves.*

8-11 *Install the shelving standards after the case has received its finish. Before nailing the standards in their dadoes, make sure that matching holes are level.*

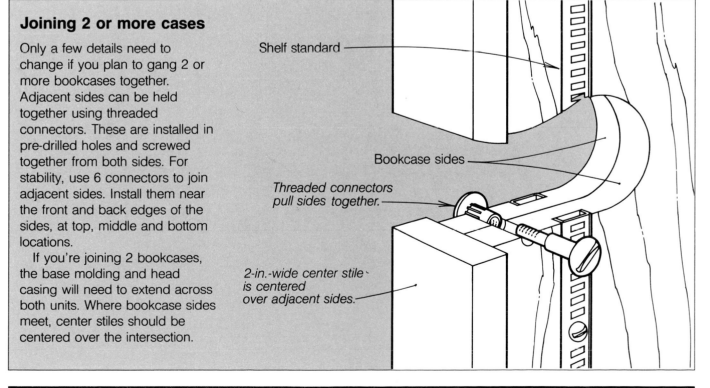

Joining 2 or more cases

Only a few details need to change if you plan to gang 2 or more bookcases together. Adjacent sides can be held together using threaded connectors. These are installed in pre-drilled holes and screwed together from both sides. For stability, use 6 connectors to join adjacent sides. Install them near the front and back edges of the sides, at top, middle and bottom locations.

If you're joining 2 bookcases, the base molding and head casing will need to extend across both units. Where bookcase sides meet, center stiles should be centered over the intersection.

Shelf standard

Bookcase sides

Threaded connectors pull sides together.

2-in.-wide center stile is centered over adjacent sides.

Chapter 9

Chest of drawers

O f the many examples of Shaker-style furniture, this chest of drawers is one of the best known. Imitations abound, some of them expensive versions made from walnut or other expensive hardwoods. On the low end, chests like this one can be made almost entirely from veneered plywood or particleboard. In most respects, the chest of drawers I've made is faithful to the antique pine chests found in furniture museums and fine antique shops.

In the old days, cabinetmakers might have chosen to cut the top and sides of the chest from a single wide board, instead of gluing up several boards as I've done here. And undoubtedly, early cabinetmakers would have cut all the dovetailed joints in this piece by hand. Luckily, we're able to use power tools to speed these and other operations.

Sides and frames

The first step in building the chest is to glue up the sides and top. I use clear, 3/4-in.-thick pine boards to make these panels. The finished dimensions of the sides are $17^{7}/_{8}$ in. by $32^{3}/_{4}$ in. The top finishes out to $41^{1}/_{2}$ in. by $18^{7}/_{8}$ in. The panels you glue up should be about 1/2 in. larger than these measurements, so that you've got room to cut edges square and smooth.

While the panels' glue is curing, you can make the 5 frames that hold the sides, top and back together. These frames also support the drawers, so they need to be strong, square, straight, and identical in size. Each frame has a pair of sides, a center piece and matching front and back pieces. All pieces are 2 in. wide. The sides and center pieces are $14^{1}/_{2}$ in. long; the front and back pieces are $38^{3}/_{4}$ in. long.

I assemble the frames using simple tongue-and-groove joints cut on the table saw with a dado cutter. First I groove the 10 front and back pieces. The dado head should be adjusted to make a 1/4-in.-wide cut. Raise the cutter 1/2 in. above the table, and set the rip fence 1/4 in. away from the cutter. Turn the saw on and mill a sample groove in scrap stock that's the same thickness as your frame members. Measure the groove to make sure it's centered in the edge. It's fine if your groove is a shade wider or narrower than 1/4 in., but it must be centered exactly. When you're sure of the rip fence's position, go ahead and mill the grooves in all 10 pieces (photo 9-1).

Both the dado head and the rip fence have to be adjusted to mill the tongues in side and center frame members (photo 9-2). The dado should be set to 1/2-in. width or greater, and lowered so that just 1/4 in. shows above the table. Clamp an auxiliary fence against the rip fence and on your side of the cutter. Adjust its location so that the fence aligns side and center pieces for a 1/2-in.-deep tongue, or tenon. To make the cut, hold the long edge of the stock against the miter gauge. A pair of cuts completes each tongue.

Before milling the sides and center pieces, test the set-up by milling a tongue in scrap stock. This tongue should mate snugly with the grooves you've milled in front and back frame members. If your test tongue is too thin, lower the dado cutter. If it's too thick, raise the cutter and make another test joint. Once the fit is right, you'll be able to mill side and center pieces (15 in all) fairly quickly.

The next step is to assemble the frames. This is repetitive work, but it has to be done accurately or the case won't fit together well. One way to make the process go quickly without sacrificing precision is to use a jig. I built mine from a small sheet of 1/2-in. plywood and

9-1 Use the table saw's rip fence as a guide when milling grooves in frame members. Adjust dado width to 1/4 in. and raise the cutter 1/2 in. above the table.

9-2 Mill tongues with the dado head raised 1/4 in. above the table and adjusted for 1/2-in. width of cut. Two passes through the cutter complete each tongue.

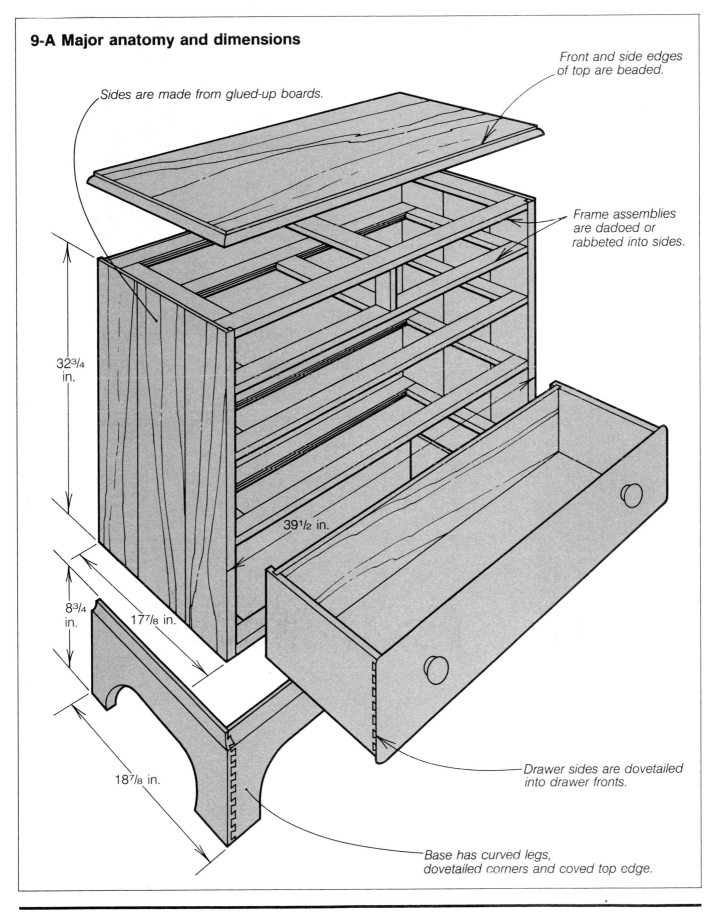

9-A Major anatomy and dimensions

Sides are made from glued-up boards.

Front and side edges of top are beaded.

Frame assemblies are dadoed or rabbeted into sides.

32³/₄ in.

39¹/₂ in.

8³/₄ in.

17⁷/₈ in.

18⁷/₈ in.

Drawer sides are dovetailed into drawer fronts.

Base has curved legs, dovetailed corners and coved top edge.

9-B Layout for side dadoes and rabbets

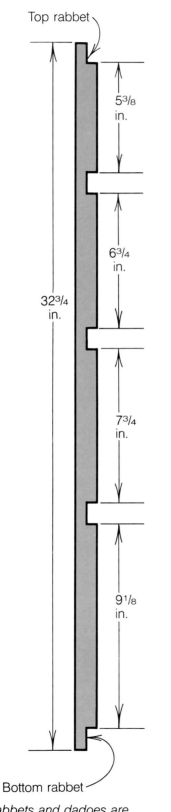

Top rabbet

5³/8 in.

6³/4 in.

32³/4 in.

7³/4 in.

9¹/8 in.

Bottom rabbet

Rabbets and dadoes are 3/4 in. wide and 3/8 in. deep.

9-3 I assemble the frames one at a time, using a jig made from plywood and scrap boards. After gluing the side and center frame members to a front or back piece, I set the assembly face-down on the jig to align and square the frame. Tongues are then nailed in grooves with 1/2-in.-brads.

several straight 1x2s that keep corners square and aligned while you nail the joints (see photo 9-3). Using a framing square, lay out the locations of the frame members. Then screw straight-edged 1x2 guide pieces to the plywood so that the frame, when assembled and square, will butt against the guide pieces. After gluing and joining a frame together, hold it against the jig's guide pieces while nailing the joints together with 1/2-in.-long wire brads. Drive a couple of nails into each joint from both sides of the frame. The brads should keep the joints square until the glue cures.

After the sides have been cut to finished size, rabbet their back edges to receive the back of the chest. The back is just 1/4 in. thick, but I make the rabbet 3/8 in. deep and 3/8 in. wide to recess the back slightly.

Now the sides can be dadoed to receive the frames. These dadoes are called "stopped dadoes" because they stop 3/4 in. short of each side's front edge. I use a table saw and dado head to cut these dadoes. Adjust the dado's width to match the thickness of your frame members, and set the cutter height at 3/8 in.

Stopped dadoes are a bit trickier to mill than regular dadoes. I use the rip fence as a guide, adjusting its location to match the layout of the dadoes (see drawing 9-B). At each of 5 rip fence settings, you'll cut matching dadoes in both sides. The sides that are run through front edge first will have to be lowered over the dado head, as shown in photo 9-4. Those that are run through back edge first will have to be lifted free just before the dado cuts to within 3/4 in. of the front edge.

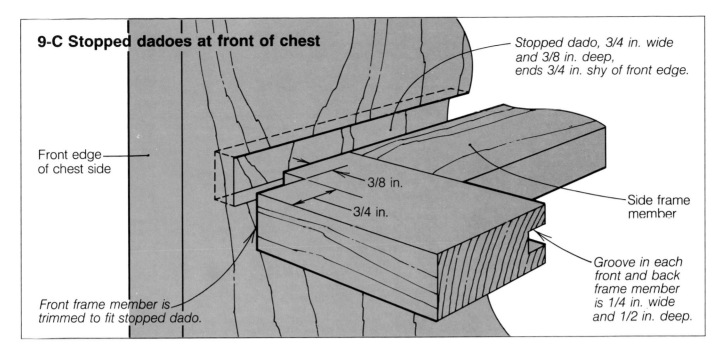

9-C Stopped dadoes at front of chest

Stopped dado, 3/4 in. wide
and 3/8 in. deep,
ends 3/4 in. shy of front edge.

Front edge
of chest side

3/8 in.

3/4 in.

Side frame
member

Groove in each
front and back
frame member
is 1/4 in. wide
and 1/2 in. deep.

*Front frame member is
trimmed to fit stopped dado.*

*9-4 Stopped dadoes are cut in two steps.
First, the sides are dadoed on the table
saw, using the rip fence as a guide.
Because the dado must stop shy of the
front edge, the side has to be lowered
over the cutter. Dado width is 3/4 in.;
depth of cut is 3/8 in.*

The stopped dadoes aren't complete until you chisel the "stopped" ends square. Use a sharp pencil and a combination square to lay out the stopped ends. Then switch to a sharp chisel —either 3/4-in. or 1/2-in. width. Using a hammer, drive the sharp edge down just inside your layout lines; then chisel from inside the dado, toward the front edge (see photo 9-5). Repeat this technique until you've reached the full 3/8-in. depth of the dado and squared the end. If you're not used to chiseling, this work can take some time. The key is to remove large chips while working inside the layout lines, and then carefully pare to the layout lines, removing delicate shavings only as the final step. With each dado, your technique will get better.

There's one small step left before sides and frames can be assembled. The front corners of every frame have to be trimmed just slightly to lap over the stopped dadoes. As shown in drawing 9-C, this

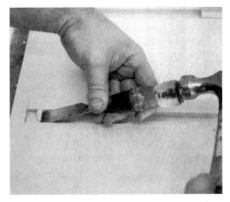

*9-5 The second step is to square up the
end of each dado with a chisel. The
square edge should stop 3/4 in. from the
side's front edge.*

9-6 *Glue and nail sides and frames together. Install the 3 center frames first. After gluing each joint, nail it fast by driving 1¹/₄-in. finishing nails at an angle, through the frame edges and into the sides of the dadoes.*

small cut-out is 3/8 in. wide and 3/4 in. deep. I make these on the table saw, raising the dado head 3/4 in. above the saw table and adjusting it to make a 3/8-in.-wide cut.

Now the frames and sides are complete, so the next step is to assemble the chest. With one side resting on the workbench, I glue and nail the 3 center frames into their respective dadoes. Be sure that the front edge of each frame is flush with the front edge of the side. Fasten the frames to the sides by driving 1¹/₄-in. finishing nails through the frame edges and into the sides of the dadoes (photo 9-6). Attach the opposite side the same way. After the 3 center frames and sides are together, you can glue and nail the top and bottom frames in place. These frames can be nailed down with 5d box nails.

As soon as frames and sides are together and before the glue sets, it's important to square up the chest and install the back (drawing 9-D). I run a bead of glue along the back edges of the frames and in the rabbets that run along the back edges of both sides. Then I position the 1/4-in.-thick back and drive 5d box nails through the back and into the top frame only. Working quickly, turn the chest upright and check the front for square by comparing diagonal measurements (photo 9-7). If you need to, rack the chest carefully until diagonals match. Check the 3 center frames to make sure they're straight, then

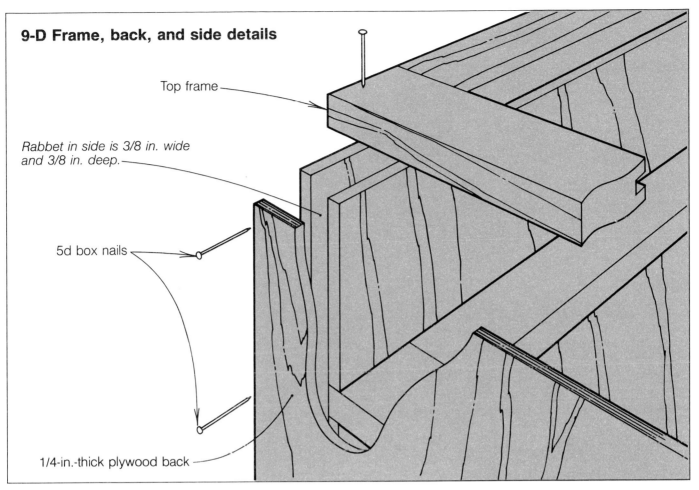

9-D Frame, back, and side details

Top frame

Rabbet in side is 3/8 in. wide and 3/8 in. deep.

5d box nails

1/4-in.-thick plywood back

finish attaching the back by driving 5d box nails into rabbets and frames.

Now cut and install the short vertical frame member that will separate the pair of small drawers at the top of the chest. Like the other frame members, this piece is 3/4 in. thick and 2 in. wide. Center it between the two upper frames, glue and screw it in place.

Building the base

The chest base has a front and two sides, and is made with dovetailed corners, curved legs and a molded top edge (see drawing 9-E). Sides and front start out as 8³/₄-in.-wide boards. If you're milling 3/8-in.-deep dadoes like I do, then the finished length of the front is 3/4 in. longer than the width of the chest (side-to-side measurement). Likewise, the finished length of the base sides will be 3/4 in. more than the depth of the chest.

It's best to mill the dovetails in base sides and front before cutting the curves for the legs. This way, if your dovetails don't come out right, you won't have wasted time cutting the legs. The dovetail jig that I use is similar to many jigs on the market. It consists of a template that's built into a right-angle clamping mechanism, which allows you to mill the tails and the pins in joining pieces in a single

9-7 Nail the back to the top frame only, then check diagonal measurements at the front of the chest to make sure it's square. If necessary, rack the chest slightly until diagonals match. Then finish nailing the back to sides and frame members.

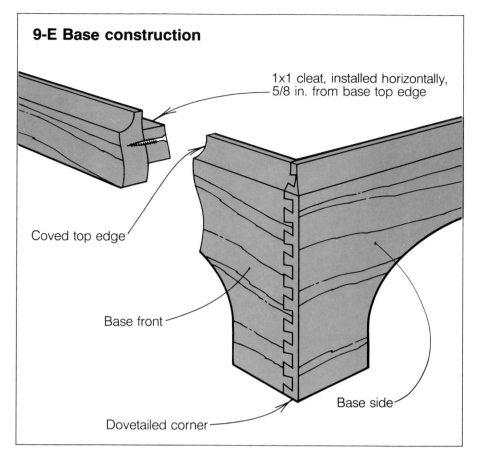

9-E Base construction

1x1 cleat, installed horizontally, 5/8 in. from base top edge

Coved top edge

Base front

Base side

Dovetailed corner

operation. The template requires a 3/8-in. dovetail bit and guide bushing to be used in the router.

Jigs like this cost between $75 and $150, and they're well worth the investment if you're planning to do any amount of cabinetry work. In terms of strength and stability, dovetail joints are far superior to any other type of joint. Properly made, a dovetail joint doesn't need to rely on glue, nails or screws to stay together; that's why you'll find dovetails on antique furniture. After a little practice with a dovetail jig, you'll be surprised at how quickly you can produce these intricate, traditional joints.

If you haven't used a jig before, be sure to read the manufacturer's instructions carefully, and mill some practice joints in scrap stock. This way, you'll learn how to clamp the stock in place and fine-tune the jig before cutting into good material. I set up my jig so that the tails are milled in the base front; the pins are milled in the sides. This lets the dovetailed corners show from the front of the chest. When you're using the jig, it's important to move the router and bushing carefully into the template's fingers (see photo 9-8). If the router base isn't flat against the template top, the dovetail bit can cut into the template instead of into the wood.

After the dovetails are milled in base front and sides, I temporarily assemble the base and trace the curves for the legs on all three pieces (photo 9-9). The pins and tails are delicate, so treat them carefully

9-8 The base has dovetailed corners that are made using a router, a 3/8-in. dovetail bit and a dovetail jig.

9-9 Dry-fit the dovetailed base corners together and trace the curved leg pattern onto the sides and front of the base.

until the joints are glued up. Once the curves are traced on front and sides, I cut them out, one at a time, on the bandsaw (photo 9-10). If you don't have a bandsaw, it's not difficult to cut these curves with a portable jigsaw.

The next step is to glue the base together. Because there's so much surface area to cover, I use a small brush to spread the glue between pins and tails. Fit the corners together carefully. If the joints are snug, as they should be, you may have to hammer them together. Be sure to use a wood mallet or a shot-filled mallet, instead of a regular hammer, which might damage the joint and mar the wood.

Now glue and screw 1x1 cleats inside the assembled base, 5/8 in. down from the top edges of sides and front. About every 8 in. or so, drive 1 1/4-in. drywall screws through the cleat and into the base. This cleat forms a ledge for the chest to rest on, as shown in drawing 9-E. It also stiffens the base slightly, a feature you'll appreciate during the next operation.

Instead of leaving a square edge along the top of the base, I mill a coved edge, using a 1/2-in. radius cove bit chucked in a router-table set-up. The coved edge doesn't hold dust like a square edge will, and it also looks better. Adjust the height of the bit and the router table's fence so that at least 1/8 in. of flat shows at the top of the cove. Test your set-up on some scrap stock first, then readjust the bit and fence if necessary. When you're ready to mill the base, run the sides through first, then the front (photo 9-11). This will leave the cleanest edge where it's most visible.

Before joining the chest to the base, give both a thorough sanding. You'll be able to do a better sanding job when these sub-assemblies are on their own. I smooth out the curves in the base using a drum sander chucked in my electric drill.

9-10 I cut the curved legs out on a bandsaw.

9-11 Set up the router table with a 1/2-in. cove bit to mill a cove in the top edge of the base. Test fence position and bit height on scrap stock first. When the set-up is right, mill the sides of the base, then the front.

Join base to chest with the chest positioned upside down. The chest should nest snugly in the base, resting against the cleats. Spread glue along the joining surfaces, and attach the cleats to the bottom frame of the chest with 1⁵/₈-in. drywall screws. For an extra measure of stability, I screw a pair of triangular braces at the back bottom corners of the chest. These braces bridge between the back edges of the base sides and the back rail of the bottom frame, as shown in photo 9-12.

Attaching the top

The top overhangs the sides and front of the chest by 1 in. I fasten it from underneath, screwing through the top frame with 1¹/₄-in. drywall screws (photo 9-13). In order to give the top room to expand and contract without pulling loose, I don't glue it down, and I use only 9 screws: 1 screw in each corner, and a screw at or near the midpoint of each frame member. The corner screws are driven in slots, rather than holes. Working the drill bit back and forth, I make these slots about 3/8 in. long and parallel with the sides of the chest (see drawing 9-F). This configuration takes into consideration that the top's movement will be greatest across the grain, rather than with it.

With the top in place, you've now got to mill a bead on its side and front edges. I use a 1/2-in. beading bit in my router. Adjust the bit's position to center the bead on the 3/4-in.-thick edge. Working from left to right, mill the side edges first, then the front. Feed the bit slowly, and take care to keep the router base flat against the top (photo 9-14).

9-12 Install the base with the chest upside down. For extra strength, glue and screw triangular braces at the back corners, joining the base sides to the bottom frame of the chest.

9-13 Attach the top by driving 1¹/₄-in. drywall screws through the top frame from inside the chest.

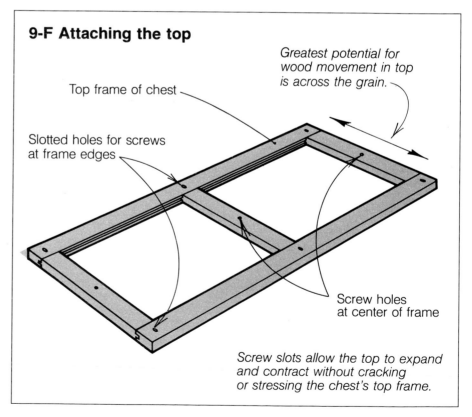

9-F Attaching the top

Greatest potential for wood movement in top is across the grain.

Top frame of chest

Slotted holes for screws at frame edges

Screw holes at center of frame

Screw slots allow the top to expand and contract without cracking or stressing the chest's top frame.

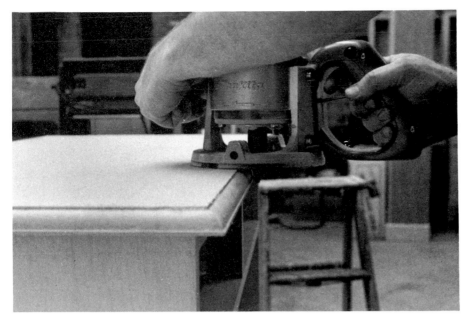

9-14 *Use a router and 1/2-in. beading bit to mill a bead along front and side edges of the top.*

Drawer construction

The drawers for this chest are designed for heavy use. Drawer sides, made with 1/2-in.-thick pine, are dovetailed into 3/4-in.-thick drawer fronts, and the fronts overlap their openings on three sides with a rounded-over lip (drawing 9-G). The first step in constructing the drawers is to cut all the parts to their finished size. On this chest, the large drawer fronts are all 38 1/4 in. long, or 1/4 in. longer than the width of the large drawer openings. The 2 small top drawers are each 18 3/4 in. long. Sides for all drawers are 17 1/4 in. long, allowing 1/4-in. clearance at the back of the chest when a drawer is closed. To calculate side widths, subtract 1/8 in. from the height of each drawer opening.

After cutting all the drawer parts to size, I rabbet the drawer fronts on their top and side edges. This rabbet is 1/4 in. wide and 1/2 in. deep, and I mill it on the table saw, with the dado head set up against a wood auxiliary fence. When all the rabbets are done, it's time to use the dovetail jig again to make the joints where drawer sides meet their fronts. In my jig, the drawer front must be clamped horizontally, under the template with the rabbet facing up. The side is clamped vertically. With this set-up, you'll mill through the side and 1/2 in. into the shoulder of the rabbet.

Once milled, the sides fit the drawer fronts only one way, so mark each side to distinguish right from left and inside face from outside face. Now set up the dado head in the table saw to mill a groove 1/2 in. wide and 1/4 in. deep. Position the rip fence 3/8 in. away from the cutter. First, dado all the sides to receive the drawer backs. Then adjust the dado's width of cut to 1/4 in., and mill the grooves in sides and drawer fronts to receive the bottoms (photo 9-15). Check the label on each side piece to make sure its dadoes are milled in the right locations.

Assuming that you've cut the backs and bottoms to size, there's one more operation to complete before you can assemble the drawers. The front edges of the drawers have to be rounded over. The lip created by the rabbeted edges is just 1/4 in. thick, so I use a 1/4-in. roundover bit to give the edges a slight curve. I set up the bit in the router table and mill the drawer edges as shown in photo 9-16. Mill a sample edge in scrap stock first to make sure the bit and fence are set up correctly. And when milling the drawer edges, always mill across the grain first so that you can finish up with the grain.

9-15 *After dovetailing drawer sides to fit into drawer fronts, dado each side to hold its bottom and back. Dado height should be 1/4 in. above the table surface. Dado width is 1/2 in. for backs and 1/4 in. for bottoms.*

9-16 *The drawer fronts have been rabbeted along top and side edges, and dovetailed to receive sides. The final step before assembly is to round over the front edges. Use a 1/4-in. roundover bit, set up in the router table. After adjusting bit height and fence position, mill the short edges of each front first, then the long edges.*

9-G Drawer construction

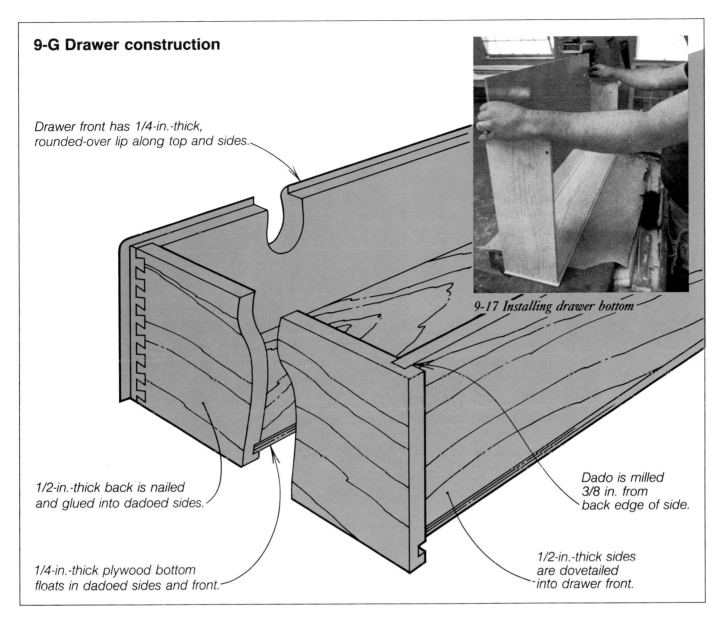

Drawer front has 1/4-in.-thick, rounded-over lip along top and sides.

9-17 Installing drawer bottom

1/2-in.-thick back is nailed and glued into dadoed sides.

1/4-in.-thick plywood bottom floats in dadoed sides and front.

Dado is milled 3/8 in. from back edge of side.

1/2-in.-thick sides are dovetailed into drawer front.

The drawers are now ready to glue up. Brush the dovetail joints with glue and assemble them first. If they need some coaxing, tap sides into fronts with a shot-filled hammer or wood mallet. Install the bottoms next (photo 9-17), and finally the backs. I let the bottom float in the dadoed sides and front, nailing it only into the back with 5d box nails. Backs should be glued and nailed in place.

This completes the chest of drawers, except for installing the drawer knobs. Simple turned wood knobs are traditional on this style of chest, but ceramic knobs also look nice, depending on the type of finish you use on the chest. To make the drawers slide smoothly, rub the bottom edges of the drawer sides with some wax.

Chapter 10

Candle stand

When we use candles today, it's usually during a power outage or a romantic dinner. But for earlier generations, candles were everyday items. The Shaker candle stand shown here was actually designed for safety and convenience. Light and compact, this tiny table could be moved around easily to provide illumination just where it was needed. The 3-legged design is wobble-proof, an important safety feature.

My candle stand is nearly identical to one that we found at Hancock Shaker Village in western Massachusetts. It's made from cherry, an excellent wood for small, delicate pieces of furniture. Maple, walnut, mahogany and ash are also good woods for this project. Pine and other softwoods aren't strong enough for the narrow curved legs that this table has.

Though it's small and it only contains 6 parts, the candle stand can be fairly challenging to build. The most difficult part of the project is cutting the sliding dovetail joints where the legs meet the column. We'll get to this later.

Turning the column

The square "blank" for the turned column starts out as a piece of cherry that measures 2⁷/₈ in. on a side and about 19 in. long. On my lathe, turning is easier if the blank is slightly longer than the finished length of the piece. Make sure your blank is free of knots or imperfections that might get in the way of a smooth turning. Then make sure the piece is square in cross-section. If it's not, you can square it up on the table saw.

The column's turned profile gives the finished table a delicate appearance without sacrificing strength (see drawing 10-B). At its top, the column flares out to form a 2-in.-diameter platform for supporting the cleat. The 3/4-in.-high, 1-in.-diameter pin at the center of the platform will fit into a hole bored in the cleat. The gentle curve below the column's top stops 4 in. from the column base. The straight lower section of the column will be dovetailed to hold the legs.

To speed the process of turning the column on the lathe, I trim a triangular section of wood off each corner of the blank. I use the bandsaw to make these cuts (photo 10-1), but you could also do the job with your table saw. The finished column will be 2³/₄ in. at its thickest point, so I trim off just enough wood to leave a rough diameter of 2⁷/₈ in.

10-1 I use the bandsaw to trim off the corners of the cherry blank for the turned column. Sawing out these 4 triangular sections will save time on the lathe.

10-A Major anatomy and dimensions

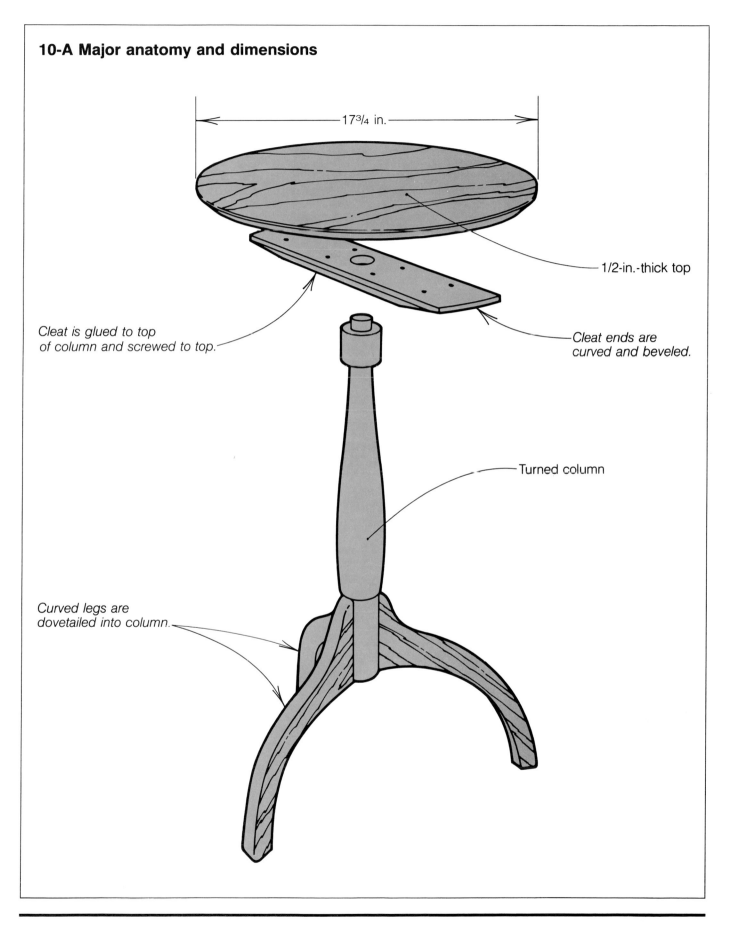

17³/₄ in.

1/2-in.-thick top

Cleat is glued to top
of column and screwed to top.

Cleat ends are
curved and beveled.

Turned column

Curved legs are
dovetailed into column.

10-B Column cross-section

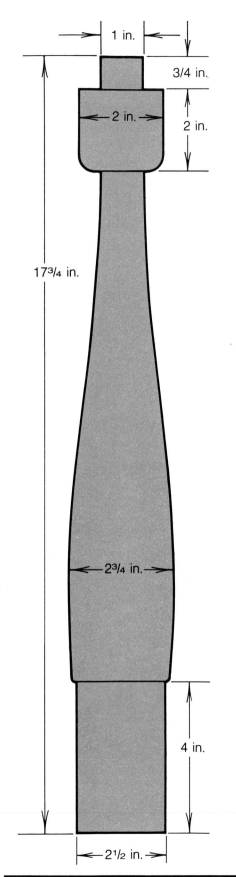

1 in.

3/4 in.

2 in.

2 in.

17³/₄ in.

2³/₄ in.

4 in.

2¹/₂ in.

10-2 With a duplicating jig installed on the lathe, the contours in a masonite template can be transferred to the turned column, using a cutting and indexing assembly.

I used a lathe duplicating jig and a masonite template of the column's profile to turn my column. If you don't have a duplicating jig, you can still turn out a duplicate of my column using standard turning tools and a good pair of calipers. As shown in photo 10-2, my jig is set up with the template located directly above the column blank. As an indexing pin moves up to the template, the cutter moves into the wood. Cutting action stops when the indexing pin contacts the template.

As in any turning project, I use a slow speed when roughing out the shape, and then speed up the lathe as I get closer to the final profile. When I've cut all that I can using the jig, I switch to an even faster speed and smooth the column with sandpaper. Start with medium-grit paper, then change to fine grit to produce a surface that's smooth enough to finish.

After removing the column from the lathe, I trim a small amount of excess from the top and bottom, giving the column its finished length of 17³/₄ in. If you have to trim the base of the column, take extra care to make this cut a square one. If the base isn't square with the axis of the column, the dovetailed grooves are likely to be off-center.

Making the legs

Using an antique candle stand as a model, I traced the shape of the legs onto some masonite and then cut out the pattern on the bandsaw. When you trace the leg's shape onto 3/4-in.-thick cherry boards, it's important to orient the grain of the cherry so that it follows the slender part of the leg as closely as possible. A leg with its grain running across this narrow width will be prone to breaking.

I use the bandsaw to cut the legs out (photo 10-3). To sand out saw marks and other irregularities, I chuck a drum sander in the drill press. Running the leg edges against this set-up really smooths them out quickly (photo 10-4). If you don't have a drill press, you can clamp each leg in a vice and use a drum sander attachment in your portable drill.

Dovetails and curves

The next step is to cut 3 dovetailed grooves in the column. The centerlines for the dovetails have to be 120 degrees apart.
To lay out these radius lines at the base of the column, I first cut a small, 120-degree-angle gauge block on the table saw. I position the block with its apex right on the center point of the base. Marking

10-3 The curved legs get cut out on the bandsaw.

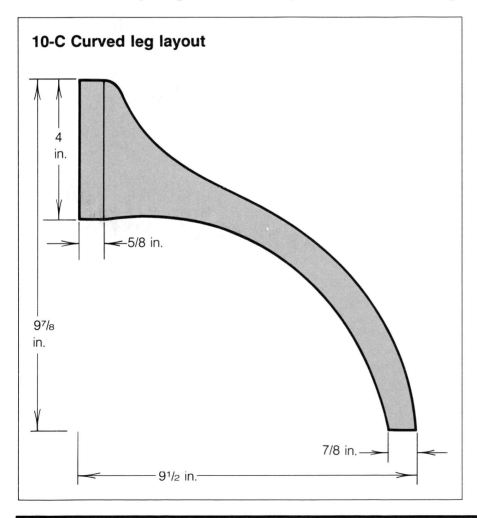

10-C Curved leg layout

4 in.

5/8 in.

9⁷⁄₈ in.

7/8 in.

9¹⁄₂ in.

10-4 A drum sander, chucked in the drill press, does a good job of smoothing the edges of each leg.

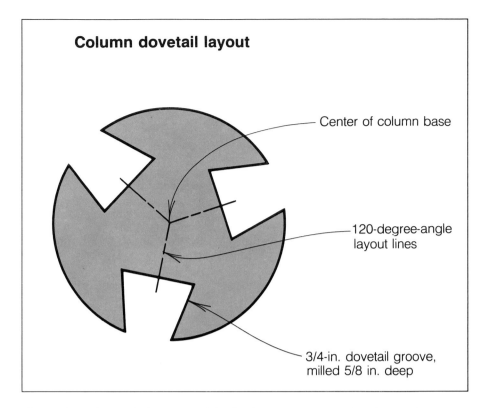

Column dovetail layout

Center of column base

120-degree-angle layout lines

3/4-in. dovetail groove, milled 5/8 in. deep

along the edges of the gauge block gives you your 120-degree layout lines.

Any kind of joinery work is difficult in a curved surface, and Colonial cabinetmakers must have struggled to dovetail the column by hand. Even with modern powertools, it's tricky to get these joints just right. The challenge is to find a way to brace the column firmly and at the same time guide the dovetail bit perfectly straight and in line with the center of the column.

The solution I came up with is a small, box-type jig that holds the column and also guides a fence attached to the router. I used 3/4-in.-thick oak to make my jig, but plywood or pine of the same thickness will also work fine. The jig's size is important. Its sides are 2³/4 in. apart. This equals the diameter of the column at its widest point, so the column will just fit between the sides. The depth inside the box is a strong 2³/4 in., or just shy of 2¹³/₁₆ in.

One end of the box is open; the other is capped with an end piece that's used for mounting and aligning the column. A rectangular cutout, centered in the top edge of this piece, provides clearance for the router bit. The centerline of the box is also marked along the bottom edge of the cutout. I align this centerline with the dovetail centerline on the column base when screwing the column to the jig (photo 10-5) with a pair of 1¹/4-in. drywall screws. Position the screws within about 1/2 in. of the column's center so that you'll have solid wood to screw into after the first dovetail is cut. To make sure that the column won't wobble in any direction, I clamp thin pieces of wood between the inside of the box and the column edges.

Now we're almost ready to dovetail the column. To keep the cut straight, the router's fence rides against one side of the jig. I chuck a carbide-tipped, 3/4-in. dovetail bit in the router, pushing the bit shank into the collet until it bottoms out. I adjust the router's fence to center the bit exactly on the dovetail's layout line. Then I adjust the depth of cut to allow the dovetail bit to penetrate 5/8 in. into the column.

With a delicate set-up and a hardwood like cherry, it would be risky to cut the dovetailed groove in a single pass. So once all the adjustments are made, I replace the dovetail bit with a 3/8-in. straight bit, and make a pass to remove most of the waste inside the groove. You shouldn't have to change the depth of cut or fence location to make this initial pass. Stop the groove about 1/8 in. shy of the ridge on the column.

As soon as the straight groove is done, chuck the dovetail bit back in the router, taking care to bottom-out the shank so that the depth of cut will remain constant for each dovetail. Mill the dovetailed groove, again stopping 1/8 in. from the ridge. Repeat this 2-cut sequence for the remaining 2 column grooves.

The legs come next. The 4-in. wide upper end of each leg must be dovetailed to slide snugly into the grooves you've just made in the column. Making these joints is a 2-step process. First the dovetails are milled on the router table, using the 3/4-in. dovetail bit; then the joints are trimmed by hand for their final fit in the column.

I make 2 passes on the router table for each dovetail (photo 10-6). Bit height and fence location must both be carefully adjusted to get these cuts right. The router-table set-up will leave square-edged shoulders on either side of the dovetail. These shoulders have to be trimmed back at an angle in order to fit against the curved column, as

10-5 The jig for cutting the column dovetails is a small box, open on the top and at one end. The notch in the end of the jig provides clearance for the dovetail bit. The router rides on the top edges of the jig, with its fence running against one side. To set up for the cut, the column base is screwed to the end of the jig. The vertical centerline of the jig should line up with the dovetail layout lines on the column base.

10-6 The height of the dovetail bit and the router table's fence location are crucial to get the leg dovetails right. Each dovetail requires 2 passes through the set-up.

10-7 I clamp a framing square against the shoulder as a guide for trimming it back to fit against the curved column. Make sure to do this trimming with a sharp blade.

10-8 To avoid the risk of ruining a good leg, it's smart to make your first dovetail in scrap stock to test the set-up of the router table and your joint-making technique.

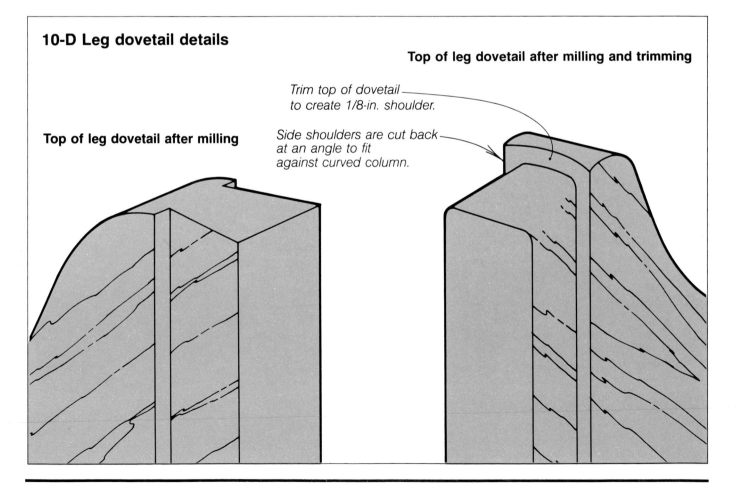

10-D Leg dovetail details

Top of leg dovetail after milling and trimming

Trim top of dovetail to create 1/8-in. shoulder.

Top of leg dovetail after milling

Side shoulders are cut back at an angle to fit against curved column.

shown in drawing 10-D. I use a sharp utility knife for this delicate work. To guide the knife for a straight cut along the shoulder, I clamp my framing square right along its edge, as shown in photo 10-7.

To finish up each joint, I use a back saw and a chisel to trim a small shoulder at the top corner of the leg, just where it meets the lip on the column. The shoulder is necessary because the dovetailed grooves don't extend all the way to the lip.

Because of all the precise cutting and fitting required for these sliding dovetail joints, it's a good idea to cut a practice joint in some scrap wood before you begin to work on the legs themselves (photo 10-8). Go through each step, beginning with the router table and finishing up with the chisel or utility knife. When you get a tight-fitting test joint, you can confidently duplicate the work in your cherry legs. Finish up each leg by rounding over its 2 top edges. I go over these edges with a 1/4-in. roundover bit in the router.

If you've made the joints well, it's very satisfying to glue the legs to the column. I apply glue to the leg dovetails, using a small brush. Then I carefully tap each dovetailed leg home in its groove (photo 10-9). With a damp sponge, I wipe off any excess glue that's found its way onto the column or legs.

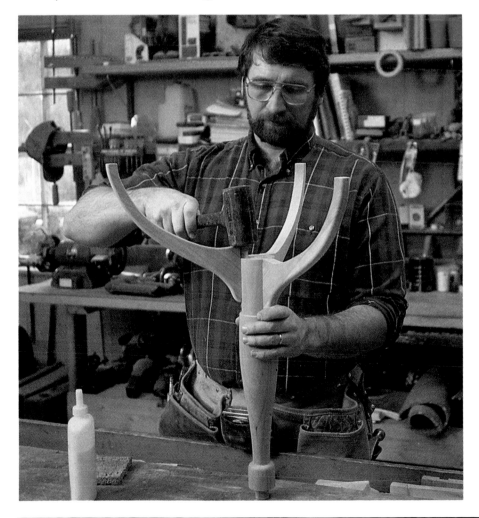

10-9 After spreading glue on the leg dovetails, I coax them into into their column grooves with a shot-filled mallet. The fit should be snug, with no need of clamps to keep the joints tight.

10-10 *A simple jig enables me to cut the curved ends of the cleat as well as the round top. First I wedge a block of wood between the guide arms of the bandsaw. Then I drive a screw through the block and into what will become the cleat's center point. The screw acts as a pivot point for cutting the curves.*

10-11 *Using the stationary belt sander, I taper the ends of the cleat.*

Cleat and top

The top isn't fastened to the column, but instead to a cleat that is glued down on the column's top pin and platform. I make the cleat first, starting with a cherry board 3³/₄ in. wide and about 18 in. long.

Instead of square-cut ends, the cleat ends are curved. It's just a slight curve, but it looks good beneath the round top of the table. The 8¹/₄-in. radius for the curved ends is half the length of the finished cleat. I cut the curves on the bandsaw, using the simple jig shown in photo 10-10. It's nothing more than a small pine board positioned flush with the saw table. I drive a screw up through the board and into the center of the cleat piece at a right angle to and 8¹/₄ in. away from the blade. The screw acts as a pivot point as I cut both ends of the cleat.

While I have the jig set up on the bandsaw, it makes sense to cut out the top of the table. I start with an 18-in.-square piece of cherry made from glued-up, 1/2-in.-thick boards. Since the finished diameter of the top is 17³/₄ in., the radius point on the jig should be located 8⁷/₈ in. away from the blade. I square a line across the underside of the top, drawing it exactly at the 9-in. mark. Then I position the top on the bandsaw table ("good" side facing up), with one edge butted against the blade and the layout line running into the blade at a right angle. Drive a screw through the radius point, up into the layout line, and you're ready to cut out the circle.

Now I go back to the cleat for a few minutes. Instead of just rounding over the curved cleat ends, I belt-sand a taper on each end (photo 10-11). To my eye, the taper looks much nicer than a simple rounded edge, and it more closely replicates the antique candle stand I found at the Shaker Village. I use a stationary belt sander to taper the cleat ends, but a portable belt sander will also do the job. There's quite a bit of wood to remove to make the taper, so start with a medium-grit or coarse-grit sanding belt. I taper each end down to the profile shown in drawing 10-E. Then I switch to an orbital sander and fine-grit paper to take out the coarse sanding marks and smooth the entire surface of the cleat.

Next I drill a 1-in.-diameter hole right in the center of the cleat so it can fit over the pin on the top of the column. I find the small screw hole from the bandsaw jig to center the drill bit. Before drilling the hole, I set up the cleat with some scrap wood underneath it to avoid splintering the cleat when the bit comes through.

Now the cleat can be glued to the column. This joint has to be strong, so I coat the column platform and pin with glue and clamp the cleat in place. While the glue is drying, I can finish up the top.

The top gets an edge treatment that's a little different. I use a router and chamfering bit along the lower edge of the top. The top edge I simply round over by hand, using fine-grit sandpaper. Then with fine-grit paper in my orbital sander, I go over the entire top until it's smooth on both sides and along every edge.

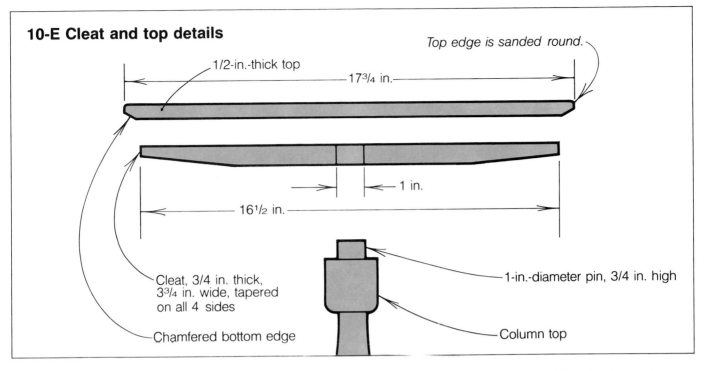

10-E Cleat and top details

Top edge is sanded round.

1/2-in.-thick top

17 3/4 in.

1 in.

16 1/2 in.

Cleat, 3/4 in. thick, 3 3/4 in. wide, tapered on all 4 sides

Chamfered bottom edge

1-in.-diameter pin, 3/4 in. high

Column top

10-12 After gluing the cleat to the column, I screw the top to the cleat. Screw holes should be pre-drilled and countersunk, and the cleat should run across the grain of the top.

Place the top upside-down on the workbench to attach the cleat and column assembly (photo 10-12). The cleat should be centered on the top's underside. As extra insurance against a warped top, the length of the cleat should run at a right angle to the grain of the top. Holding the cleat in place, I pre-drill all the screw holes to fasten it to the top. About 4 screws on either side of the hole should be enough. I counterbore each hole slightly to make sure the 1-in.-long screws stay hidden. Take care not to drill through the top's good side.

Chapter 11

Hutch

Before plumbing, central heating, refrigerators and plastic laminate transformed the kitchen (and every other room in the house), every American home had at least one cupboard. Everyday dishes and pans were stored in the kitchen cupboard, while a separate dining room cupboard served as both storage and display space for the family's finer china.

The type of cupboard I've built here is often called a hutch. With 3 drawers over 3 doors and an upper cabinet with 3 shelves, this is a large piece of furniture. To scale it down, you could make a 2-door, 2-drawer version using the same joinery and techniques described here. Another option is to build just the hutch base, without the upper cabinet, and use it as a sideboard. I'll show you how to build the base first.

Making the top and sides

The top and sides of the hutch base are pine panels made from glued-up, 3/4-in.-thick boards. Choose good stock to make these panels free of warps, checks and loose knots. The finished dimensions of the sides are 16³/₄ in. by 34¹/₄ in. The top finishes out to 18¹/₄ in. by 55¹/₂ in. When you glue up the panels for these parts, make them at least 1/2 in. longer and wider than their finished dimensions so that you'll have room to square up the edges.

While the glue is setting, I make the 2 frames that join both sides together. The upper frame serves as a base for attaching the top, while the lower frame becomes a drawer runner assembly. Like the frame assemblies used to make the chest of drawers (chapter 9), these frames are made by joining grooved front and back members with tongued side and center members (see drawing 11-B). The front and back members arc 2 in. wide and 53¼ in. long. The side members are 2 in. wide and 13⅜ in. long, and the center members (used on the lower frame only) are 3½ in. wide and 13⅜ in. long.

The tongues and grooves in frame members are milled on the table saw, using the dado head. I use the same set-up described in chapter 9, when making the frames for the chest of drawers (see photos 9-1 and 9-2). When all the joints have been milled, glue and nail the frames together. I tap the joints together with a shot-filled hammer, and nail them with 1/2-in. brads (photo 11-1).

The sides of the hutch base have to be rabbeted and dadoed to hold the frames and shelves. I adjust the dado head in the table saw to cut 3/4 in. wide and 3/8 in. deep. Use the rip fence to guide each side as you mill across the grain. You'll have to adjust the fence position to match the layout of the dadoes, which is shown in drawing 11-C. Notice that the top edge of each side gets a rabbet instead of a dado. The back edge of each side also needs to be rabbeted to hold the 1/4-in.-thick plywood back. I mill this rabbet 3/8 in. wide and 3/8 in. deep to recess the back slightly.

The last cuts to complete the sides are curved ones. Using a pattern cut in a scrap piece of wood, I trace a pointed curve along the bottom edge of each side. These cut-outs transform the square bottom edges into legs, giving the base a lighter appearance. To center the leg curves onto the sides, remember that the face frame will add an extra 3/4 in. to the width of the front leg. Cut out the curves with a portable jigsaw (photo 11-2).

Cut the shelves from a sheet of 3/4-in.-thick plywood. I use common A/C grade plywood, making sure that the "A" side of the shelf faces up. The bottom shelf has the same outside dimensions as the frame assemblies (17⅜ in. by 53¼ in.). The center shelf is an inch narrower, to allow for a solid wood edge strip.

11-1 The lower frame for the hutch base is a 6-piece assembly. Tongues milled in the short side and center pieces are glued and nailed into grooves in front and back frame members.

11-A Major anatomy and dimensions

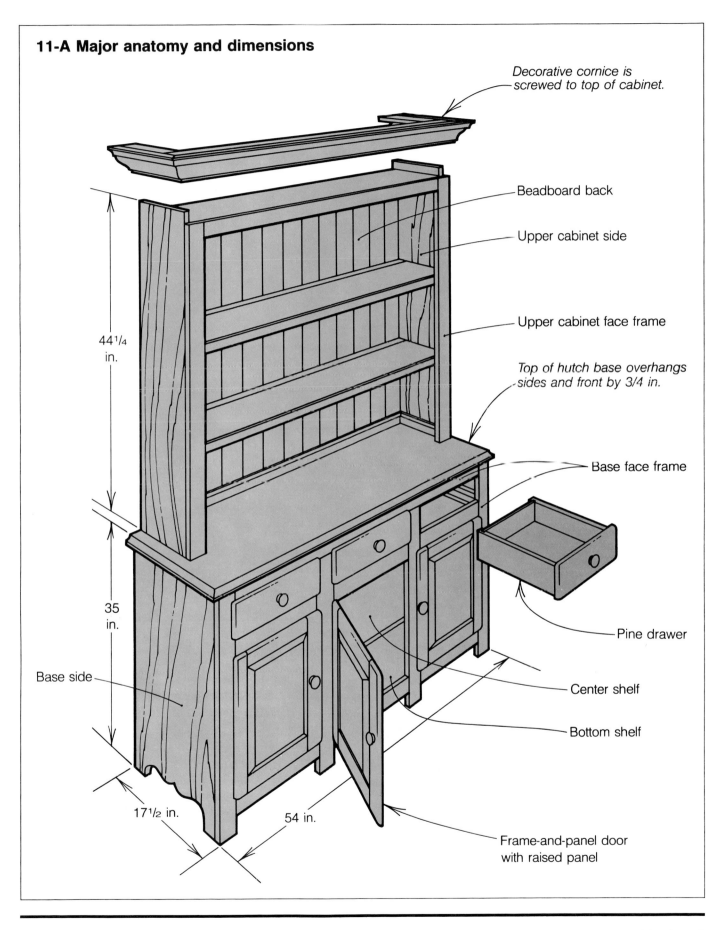

Decorative cornice is screwed to top of cabinet.

Beadboard back

Upper cabinet side

Upper cabinet face frame

Top of hutch base overhangs sides and front by 3/4 in.

Base face frame

Pine drawer

Center shelf

Bottom shelf

Frame-and-panel door with raised panel

44¹/₄ in.

35 in.

Base side

17¹/₂ in.

54 in.

11-B Frames and shelves for the hutch base

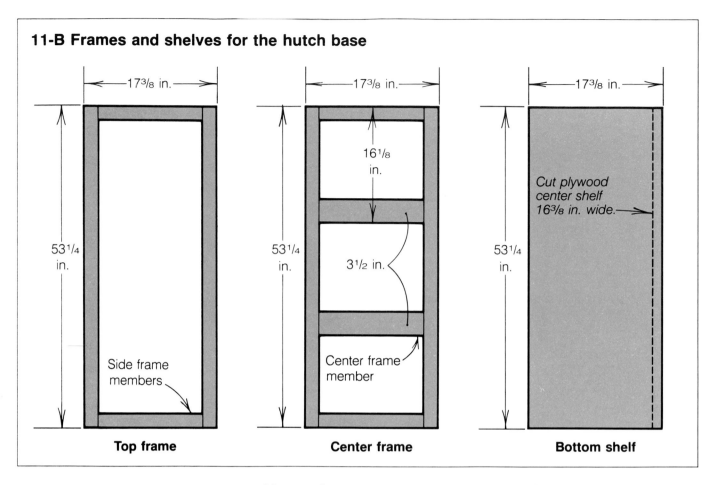

Top frame — 17³/₈ in. — 53¹/₄ in. — Side frame members

Center frame — 17³/₈ in. — 53¹/₄ in. — 16¹/₈ in. — 3¹/₂ in. — Center frame member

Bottom shelf — 17³/₈ in. — 53¹/₄ in. — Cut plywood center shelf 16³/₈ in. wide.

Now you're ready to assemble the "carcase," or structural case, of the hutch. I start by gluing the lower frame and the 2 plywood shelves into their dadoes in one side of the hutch (photo 11-3). Remember when installing the middle shelf to leave room for the 1-in.-wide pine edge strip at the front of the hutch. To hold the frame and shelves in place while the glue dries, drive 6d finish nails through the frame or plywood and into the shoulders of the dadoes.

When the shelves and middle frame are glued and nailed in place, I attach the opposite side of the hutch. The top frame can be installed with the hutch upright, resting on its legs. But before installing it, I attach the upper drawer guides to the front and back frame members. As shown in drawing 11-E, these 1-in.-wide guides run from front to back, and keep the drawers from tipping out of their openings. Using 1⅝-in. drywall screws, fasten the 3 upper guides to the underside of the frame. Then glue and screw the frame to the sides.

As soon as the last frame is down, you can attach the 1/4-in. plywood back. Before gluing and nailing the back in place, I check the carcase to make sure the sides are square with shelves and frames. Finally, use glue and 6d finish nails to attach a 1-in.-wide pine lip to the front edge of the middle shelf (photo 11-4). This narrow trim hides and protects the plywood edge. Installing the face frame will cover the front edge of the bottom shelf.

11-2 *After tracing a pointed curve pattern onto both sides, I use a portable jigsaw to cut out the legs.*

11-3 *Glue and nail the lower frame and plywood shelves into their dadoes, one side at a time.*

11-4 *The plywood edge of the center shelf is covered by a pine lip 3/4 in. thick and 1 in. wide. Glue and nail the lip in place with 4d finish nails.*

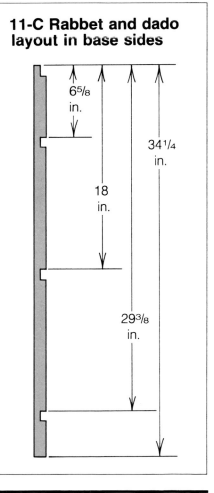

11-C Rabbet and dado layout in base sides

$6^5/_8$ in.

$34^1/_4$ in.

18 in.

$29^3/_8$ in.

Making the face frame and attaching the top

The face frame is made from 3/4-in.-thick pine, ripped into strips 1³/4 in. wide. The vertical members are called "stiles"; horizontal pieces are called "rails." Stiles and rails are joined together with lap joints.

The hutch face frame has 4 stiles and 3 rails, so there are quite a few lap joints to cut. The joinery details are shown in drawing 11-D. The 2 side stiles have their "laps" facing in. The 2 lowermost rails have their laps facing out. Center stiles and the top rail have laps that face both ways. Careful layout is important to make sure the joints in each piece are cut so that they face the right way. I label each frame member, and position all frame members over the carcase when laying out the joints (photo 11-5).

I cut the lap joints on the radial arm saw, using a dado head adjusted for maximum width of cut. The depth of cut has to be carefully adjusted so that the dado removes half the thickness of the frame

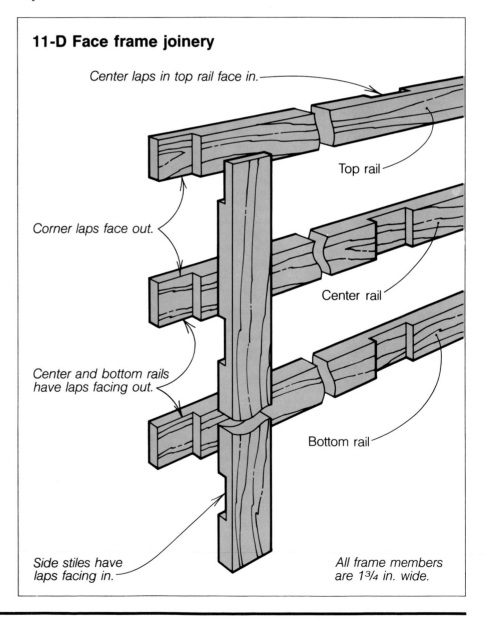

11-D Face frame joinery

Center laps in top rail face in.

Top rail

Corner laps face out.

Center rail

Center and bottom rails have laps facing out.

Bottom rail

Side stiles have laps facing in.

All frame members are 1³/4 in. wide.

11-6 *I cut all the lap joints using the dado head on the radial arm saw.*

11-5 *Accuracy is crucial in laying out the lap joints in the face frame. The surest way to get the layout right is to mark up the pieces while they're in place on the front of the base.*

member, or 3/8 in. if your stock is 3/4 in. thick. I mill a test joint in 2 pieces of scrap wood to make sure the depth of cut is right. Cut each joint by making repeated passes with the dado until you've removed all the material inside your layout lines (photo 11-6).

I glue the face frame together, and drive a pair of 1/2-in., flat-head screws through the back of each lap joint to pull it tight. As soon as the frame is complete, you can glue and nail it to the base (use 6d finish nails). Then set the nails, and give the frame a thorough sanding with medium-grit paper (photo 11-7).

Before attaching the top of the hutch base, the lower drawer guides need to be screwed to the lower frame. Each lower guide (there are 4 in all) should extend 1/16 in. beyond the face frame stiles, as shown in drawing 11-E. When you screw these guides to the lower frame, make sure they're square with the face frame.

The top of the hutch is attached the same way as the top of the chest of drawers (chapter 9). Make sure the top overlaps the sides and front of the base evenly, then drive 1¼-in. screws through the top frame and into the top. To allow for expansion and contraction of the top, I make slots for the screws at the edges of the frame, as shown in drawing 9-F. To finish off the top, I give it a decorative edge, using a 1/4-in. "ogee" bit chucked in the router.

11-7 *After gluing and nailing the face frame to the hutch, I go over it with the orbital sander, using medium-grit sandpaper.*

Doors and drawers

The doors for this hutch are traditional frame-and-panel doors with

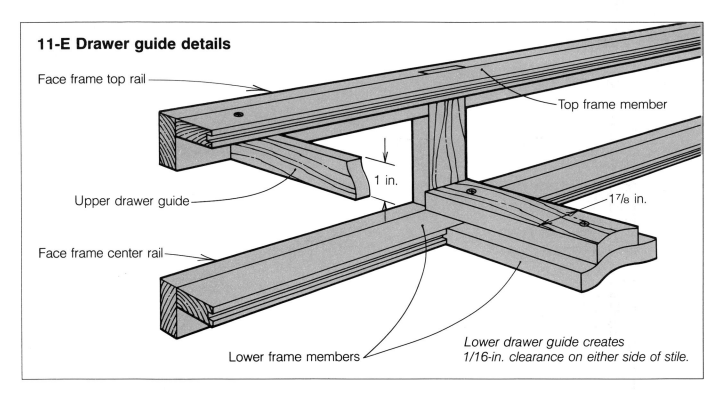

11-E Drawer guide details

Face frame top rail

Top frame member

1 in.

Upper drawer guide

1⁷/₈ in.

Face frame center rail

Lower frame members

Lower drawer guide creates 1/16-in. clearance on either side of stile.

11-8 Raised panels for the doors are milled on the radial arm saw, using a molding head and panel cutters.

raised panels. Like the face frame, the door frames consist of vertical stiles and horizontal rails. The inside edges of the frame are grooved to hold the panel. Because these are "overlay" doors, they're slightly larger than their openings. I'll explain how to size the door frames below.

Instead of joining stiles and rails with traditional mortise-and-tenon joints, I fasten the frame together by driving screws in pocket holes that are drilled in the rails. I start by cutting the 2-in.-wide stiles and rails for all 3 doors to their finished lengths. To do this, add 1/2 in. to the height of the door opening to get stile length. Subtract 3¹/₂ in. from the width of the door opening to get rail length. If you've made the hutch face frame accurately, all 3 door openings should measure the same.

The next step is to mill grooves for the panel along the inside edges of stiles and rails. I set up a 3/8-in. straight bit in the router table and raise it 7/16 in. above the table. Then I adjust the fence so that the groove will be centered exactly in the stock. Mill grooves along the full length of the rails. Stile grooves need to start and stop 1¹/₂ in. from the ends of the stiles. To mill these grooves, lower each stile firmly and carefully over the bit, then lift the stile free of the bit when you've milled to within 1 in. of the end.

Now you can make the raised panels that fit into the door frames. I glue up a pair of 1x8 pine boards to make each panel. The finished size of the panel should allow it to "float" in its frame, with 1/16 in. of clearance between each panel edge and the bottom of its groove. If panel grooves are 7/16 in. deep, add 1 in. to the width of the frame opening and 1 in. to the height of the opening to get the panel's dimensions.

I raise the panels with the radial arm saw, using a molding head

11-9 *I use the pocket hole jig to drill the rails of the hutch doors, so that they can be glued and screwed to the stiles. The frame members have already been grooved to accept their panels.*

The pocket hole jig

Screws driven in pocket holes are a fast alternative to mortise-and-tenon joinery. I had my pocket hole jig made up at a machine shop. It's nothing more than a piece of aluminum stock with a 3/8-in.-diameter hole bored through one end at a 15-degree angle.

To use the jig, clamp it firmly to the stock so that the hole is aimed into the joint. Using a 3/8-in., brad-point bit, drill to within 3/8 in. of the joining edge. Tape wrapped around the bit acts as a depth gauge. Always use pan-head screws in pocket holes; they're less likely to split the wood.

equipped with panel cutters (photo 11-8). It's wise to mill the panel edges in stages, making your first passes with the cutters lowered just slightly into the stock. With each panel, be sure to mill across the grain first, then with the grain. Lower the cutters until you've "raised" panels with an edge thickness of 3/8 in.

If you're able to use the pocket hole jig to drill out screw holes, joining the door frames together is very easy (see sidebar). Each rail gets a single pocket hole. After smearing the rail ends with glue and assembling a frame around its panel, I drive #6 1 1/4-in. pan-head screws to pull rails tight against stiles.

When the doors are assembled, I round over their outer edges, using a router and 3/8-in. roundover bit. Then I go back to the router table and rabbet the inner edges of each door. Adjust the bit and fence to cut 3/8 in. deep and 3/8 in. wide. Now you're finally ready to mount the doors. The hinges I use on this hutch are called semi-concealed casework hinges, and they're designed for overlay doors where the rabbeted edge is 3/8 in. by 3/8 in. (photo 11-10). I chose simple brass handles to compliment the brass-plated hinges. To keep the doors closed, you'll have to install either magnetic or spring-type catches.

The drawers for the hutch base are nearly identical to the drawers I built for the chest of drawers (chapter 9). The 1/2-in.-thick drawer sides are dovetailed into the 3/4-in.-thick drawer fronts. The fronts for my hutch are 5 1/2 in. wide and 16 1/8 in. long, or 1/2 in. larger than the face frame openings. The sides are 4 3/4 in. wide and 16 3/4 in. long. Drawer backs (cut from 1/2-in.-thick pine) are 4 1/8 in. wide and 15 in. long. The 1/4-in.-thick plywood drawer bottoms are 14 15/16 in. wide and 16 3/16 in. long.

11-10 *Overlay doors like these can be hung using semi-concealed casework hinges, which don't require mortises.*

11-11 I round over the edges on the door fronts on the router table, with a 1/4-in. roundover bit. This drawer front has already been rabbeted to overlay its opening, dovetailed to receive its sides, and dadoed to hold the bottom.

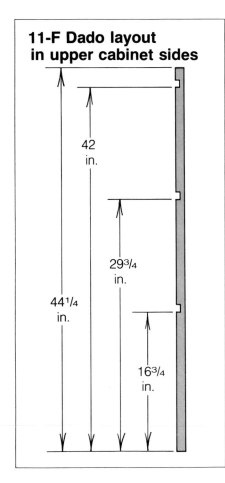

11-F Dado layout in upper cabinet sides

42 in.

29³/₄ in.

44¹/₄ in.

16³/₄ in.

The first step in making the drawers is to mill a 3/8-in. by 3/8-in. rabbet along the inside edges of the drawer fronts. I do this on the router table, with the same set-up I used on the hutch doors. Next, I pair up drawer fronts and sides in the dovetail jig, and mill the dovetails that join both parts together.

Drawer sides and fronts have to be dadoed for their 1/4-in. plywood bottoms. Each side must also be dadoed to hold its back. I do all this milling on the table saw, using the dado cutter. Finally, I go back to the router table to round over all 4 edges of each drawer front (photo 11-11). The drawers can now be assembled. I use a small brush to spread glue on the dovetail joints and tap them together with the shot-filled hammer. Then I slide in the bottom and glue and nail the back in place.

Building the upper cabinet

The upper half of the hutch is a simple set of shelves with a face frame, a 3/4-in.-thick back and a decorative cornice. The 1x8 "beadboard" stock that I use to make the cabinet back isn't available at all lumber yards. If you have trouble finding beadboard, you can substitute common tongue-and-groove boards. With a molding head and beading cutters, it's even possible to mill your own beadboard from standard 1x stock.

I start by cutting sides and shelves from clear, straight 1x10 stock. The sides are 9 in. wide and 44¹/₄ in. long. The shelves are 8¹/₄ in. wide and 52³/₄ in. long. After cutting the shelves to length, I mill a plate groove along the full length of each shelf, using a 1/4-in. round-nose bit in the router. I adjust the depth of cut to 1/4 in., and use a fence on the router to run the groove 2 in. from the back edge of each shelf.

Next, I dado the sides to hold the shelves. Whether you do this on the table saw or radial arm saw, the dadoes should be 3/4 in. wide and 3/8 in. deep. Shelf spacing, or dado layout, is shown in drawing 11-F. The back edge of each side should be rabbeted so that the beadboard fits into the rabbet. Mill these rabbets 3/8 in. deep and 3/4 in. wide.

With glue and 6d finish nails, I assemble sides and shelves (photo 11-12). The front edges of the shelves should be flush with the front edges of the sides. Like the hutch base, the shelves also get a face frame, but this one is a little easier to build because there are just 2 stiles and a single rail. The frame members are 1⁷/₈ in. wide, and the rail laps under the stiles. The top edge of the rail is flush with the top face of the shelf that it's nailed against.

The next step is to make and install a small base molding. Instead of using a stock molding from the lumber yard, I milled my own on the router table, using a 1/4-in. Roman ogee bit. The finished molding is 1⁷/₈ in. high. As shown in drawing 11-G, this molding is installed in three pieces, with mitered corners where the pieces meet. The short end pieces are glued and nailed (with 4d finish nails) inside the bottom ends of the shelf sides. The long piece extends all the way across the back of the shelves, connecting both sides. In addition to creating a graceful transition between the 2 parts of the hutch, the back molding serves as an anchoring point for the beadboard back, which is screwed into it.

The upper cabinet needs to be attached to the hutch base in some way, and I use the traditional method: short dowel pins that extend from the bottom edges of the upper cabinet into holes in the top of the hutch base (see drawing 11-G). Each side of the upper cabinet gets a pair of 3/8-in.-diameter dowel pins. I also locate 2 pins along the back

11-12 Assemble the upper cabinet by gluing and nailing shelves into dadoes milled in the sides.

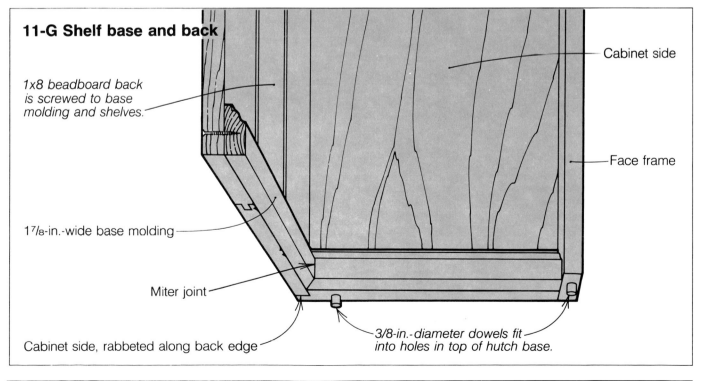

11-G Shelf base and back

1x8 beadboard back is screwed to base molding and shelves.

1⁷⁄₈-in.-wide base molding

Miter joint

Cabinet side, rabbeted along back edge

3/8-in.-diameter dowels fit into holes in top of hutch base.

Cabinet side

Face frame

of the upper cabinet. The pins are 1 in. long, and extend 1/2 in. into each part of the completed hutch.

Once the upper cabinet has been pinned to the base, the back can be installed. Working from one side to the other, I drive 1 1/4-in. drywall screws through each piece of beadboard and into the back edge of each shelf. As each piece of beadboard goes up, check the shelves to make sure they stay straight.

Making the cornice

Like the bookcase, these shelves have a cornice, a feature you'll find on many traditional furniture pieces. This cornice is built up in several layers, the most visible one being the 3 5/8-in. crown molding that runs around the top, mitered at the corners. I designed the entire cornice assembly to be detachable. This way, the cornice can get moved on its own when you move your hutch, so it's less likely to be damaged.

The first part of the cornice to make is a band 2 1/2 in. wide and 3/4 in. thick. Technically, you could call this backer piece a "reveal," since it builds the cornice out from the sides and front of the shelves, and creates a shadow line beneath the crown molding. The 3-piece reveal should be mitered at the top corners of the shelves, with the front piece overlapping the face frame's top rail by 1/4 in. (see drawing 11-H).

Attach the reveal by driving 1 1/4-in. drywall screws through the cabinet sides and into the reveal side pieces. The front reveal piece is attached to 3 backer blocks — one at each corner and a block at the center. These blocks are screwed into the face frame's top rail.

Once screwed to the top of the cabinet, the reveal serves as a base for the angled cleat that's attached next (photo 11-13). Like the reveal, the cleat consists of 3 mitered pieces, each one 3/4 in. thick and 1 1/8 in. wide. The 40-degree angle ripped along the bottom edge of the cleat matches the angle that the back of the crown molding makes when it's installed against the reveal.

Now the crown molding can be mitered and installed. It's best to miter the long front piece of molding first, then miter the side pieces, leaving the square ends long so that they can be trimmed exactly once the miters fit just right. I use a power miter box to cut my 45-degree angles, but you can also cut these miters by hand if you have a conventional miter box. Either way, it takes time to set up the molding in the box so that the miters are oriented the right way. As shown in photo 11-14, I clamp a small fence to my miter box to hold the molding at the proper angle.

When all three pieces of crown molding are cut, they can be glued and nailed to the reveal pieces and angled cleats. Use 4d finish nails. I also glue and nail the miter joints together, taking care not to split the wood (photo 11-15). Finally, I install angled blocks between the cleat and the top part of the molding. Gluing the molding to these pieces (shown in photo 11-16 and drawing 11-H) keeps the top edge of the molding even across the front and along both sides.

11-13 Attach the angled cleat to the reveal with 1 1/4-in. drywall screws. The cleat and the reveal are both 3-piece assemblies with mitered corners.

11-14 A wood fence, clamped to the saw table, helps to keep the cornice molding positioned as the miter cut is made.

11-15 I use 4d finish nails to pull the molding's miter joints tight while the glue sets. Nails should be set carefully and then filled after finish has been applied.

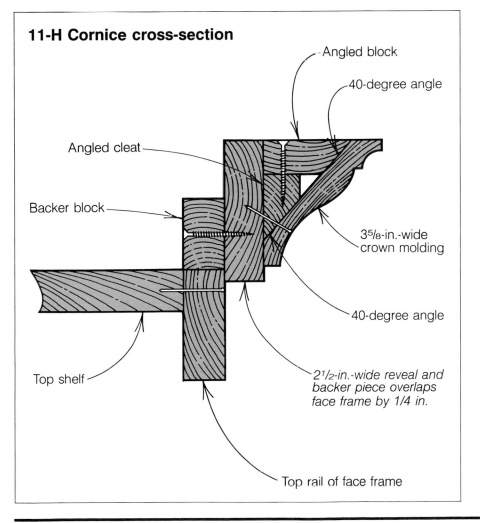

11-H Cornice cross-section

Angled block

40-degree angle

Angled cleat

Backer block

$3^5/_8$-in.-wide crown molding

40-degree angle

$2^1/_2$-in.-wide reveal and backer piece overlaps face frame by 1/4 in.

Top shelf

Top rail of face frame

11-16 Install angled blocks to keep the top edge of the molding even and strengthen the upper part of the cornice. Fasten the blocks to the top edge of the angled cleat and to the back of the molding.

Chapter 12

Slant-front desk

The slant-front desk is an enduring example of how early cabinetmakers combined practicality with fine craftsmanship. When closed, the desk takes up very little space. But with the front opened and resting on a pair of slide-out supports, this diminutive piece of furniture becomes a miniature office. There's a surprisingly large work surface, and against the back of the cabinet, dividers and small drawers create an ample storage area.

You'll find other slant-front desk designs that include a full chest of drawers beneath the desk cabinet. I like the "desk-on-frame" design shown here because it leaves room beneath the cabinet for a chair to be pushed in. Another advantage is that the upper part of the desk, which I call the cabinet, can easily be detached from the base if you ever need to move the desk.

I examined several old slant-front desks before designing my own version. My desk has many of the features you'll find in an antique slant-top. The legs of the base are tapered, and meet the rails with mortise-and-tenon joints that are pegged with dowels. The desk top is dovetailed into the sides, and the supports for the front slide in a screw-and-slot assembly. The major difference between my desk and many older versions is the size of the cabinet. I changed the cabinet's proportions slightly so that the vertical compartments at the back of my desk will accommodate a full-size sheet of paper.

Make the panels first

The sides, front, inner work surface, top and compartment dividers are all made from glued-up maple boards. Before you begin any other part of the project, it's a good idea to glue up enough panels to make all these parts. While the glue is setting, you can go on to other operations.

I go through my supply of maple carefully to make the panels, selecting clear, straight pieces. Each panel should be made at least 1/2 in. larger than the finished dimensions of the part that will be cut from it. I cut both cabinet sides from a panel 18½ in. wide and 42 in. long.

The panel for the inner work surface can be made 20 in. wide and 34 1/4 in. long. The "rough" size of my top panel is 10 in. by 34 1/2 in., and the front's panel can be 16 in. wide and 32 in. long. Apply the same oversize rule for the compartment dividers, but glue them up from 1/2-in.-thick boards.

Building the base

The base is much easier to build than the upper cabinet of the desk. I start by making the legs. These are cut from square stock, 1 5/8 in. on a side. Finished length is 24 1/2 in. The legs are tapered, but before cutting the tapers, I mill a pair of mortises in each leg to hold the tenoned rails. Each mortise begins 1/2 in. down from the top of the leg and needs to be 2 in. long, 3/8 in. wide and 7/8 in. deep. By locating the mortise 1/4 in. away from the front face of the leg, I create a slight reveal (1/16 in.) where the rail joins the leg.

To mill the mortises, I set up a hollow-chisel mortising bit in the drill press. A fence keeps the stock aligned while I plunge the bit. Hold-downs on the mortising assembly enable me to pull the bit free after reaching the full depth of the mortise (photo 12-1). If you don't have a hollow-chisel bit, you can drill out these mortises with a 3/8-in. bit and then chisel the edges square by hand.

Tapering the legs is the next step. The legs for this desk are tapered on their 2 inside faces only. The tapers start 3 3/4 in. from the top of the leg, leaving a 7/8-in. square to bear on the floor (drawing 12-B). I taper the legs using a jig that I made from a couple of straight boards and a hinge. As shown in photo 12-2, the straight side of the jig runs

12-1 A hollow-chisel mortising bit makes quick work of mortising the legs. I clamp a fence to the drill press table to keep the leg aligned with the bit.

12-2 The taper jig has a straight side that runs against the rip fence, and a slanted side that holds the stock. Taper only the 2 inside faces of each leg.

12-A Major anatomy and dimensions

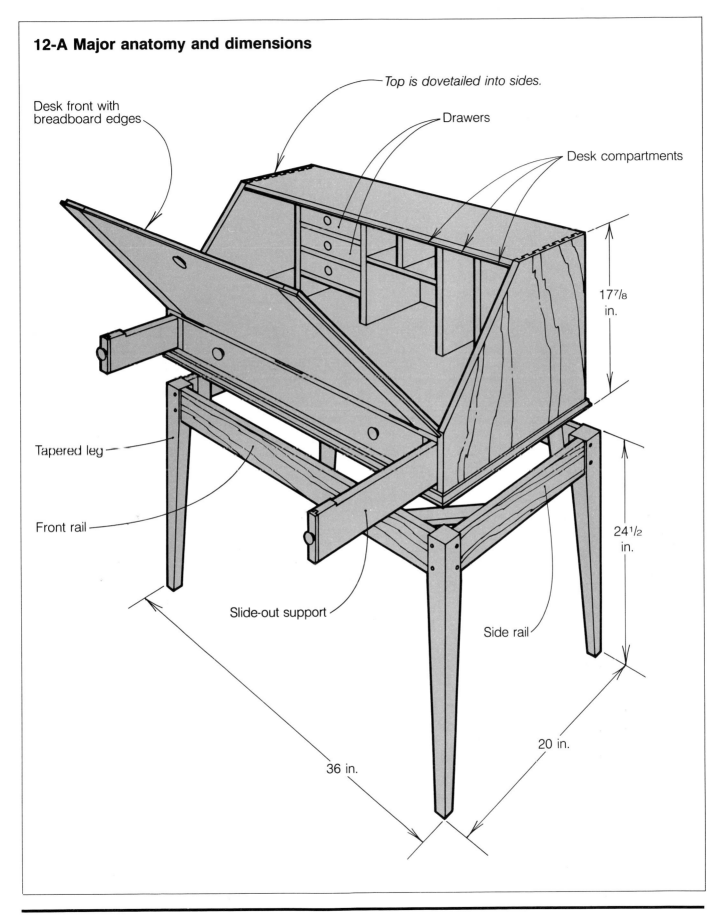

Desk front with breadboard edges

Top is dovetailed into sides.

Drawers

Desk compartments

17⅞ in.

Tapered leg

Front rail

24½ in.

Slide-out support

Side rail

36 in.

20 in.

12-B Tapered leg details

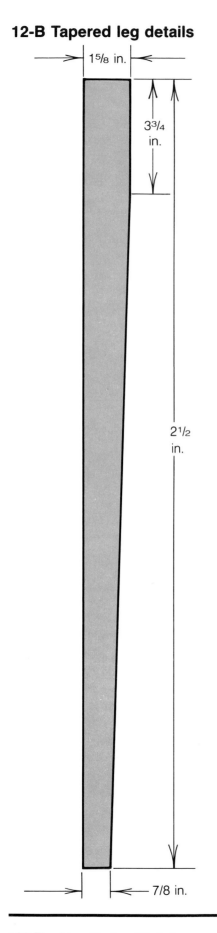

1⁵/₈ in.

3³/₄ in.

2¹/₂ in.

7/8 in.

against the rip fence. The slanted side holds the stock. The degree of taper is adjusted with a simple screw and arm assembly.

To set up the jig for this taper, you have to adjust both the rip fence position and the jig's slanted arm so that the cut will start 3³/₄ in. down from the top of the leg and finish leaving 7/8 in. of wood between the blade and the jig. Before I run the maple legs through the set-up, I test it on some scrap stock that's identical in thickness and length. It's much better to make your mistakes during a "test run" than to ruin a leg that's already been mortised.

Especially with maple, slanted cuts can leave burn marks in the wood. As soon as the tapers are cut, I go over each leg with the belt sander and a fine-grit sanding belt. Then I switch to an orbital sander and fine-grit paper. Finally, I ease all the edges by hand with fine-grit paper. When you're done, the legs should be smooth enough to finish.

The rails come next. Because of maple's strength, rail width can be held to 3 in. The finished length of the front and back rails is 34¹/₂ in. long. Side rails should be cut 18¹/₂ in. long. The tenons are 2 in. wide, 3/8 in. thick and 7/8 in. long (see drawing 12-C). I use the table saw for all the tenoning work. The long shoulders are cut first, with the blade raised 3/16 in. above the table and a wood gauge block clamped to the rip fence to align the cut. Then I raise the blade 1/2 in. above the table and turn the rails on edge to remove 1/2 in. from the top and bottom of each tenon (photo 12-3). The cheeks are cut last by running the rails on end through the saw (photo 12-4). Blade height should be 7/8 in., and the rip fence needs to be set 9/16 in. away from the blade.

Now you can assemble the base. I glue the long tenons in their mortises first and clamp them together. Then with a 1/4-in., brad-point bit, I drill through the mortise and tenon so that the joint

12-3 *A wood gauge block (clamped to the rip fence) and the miter gauge align the shoulder cuts for each tenon. Successive passes through the blade remove the waste at the top and bottom of the tenon.*

12-4 *To complete the tenon, make a pair of cheek cuts with the rail held on end. Use the rip fence to guide first one face of the rail, then the other, through the blade. For safety, push the stock with a scrap piece of wood.*

can be pegged with a pair of 1/4-in. dowels. Because of the strength of modern wood glue (something that early cabinetmakers couldn't rely on), it's not crucial to peg these mortise-and-tenon joints. But the pegs definitely give the desk a more traditional look, and once a joint is pegged, its clamps can be removed.

Layout for the peg holes is shown in drawing 12-C. Masking tape, wrapped around the bit 3/4 in. up from its tip, tells me when each hole is deep enough. I drive 1-in.-long dowels into the holes after dabbing them with glue. The dowels should stand proud by about 1/4 in., so that you can sand them flush when the glue dries. As soon as the long rails and legs are together, I glue the short rails to the legs,

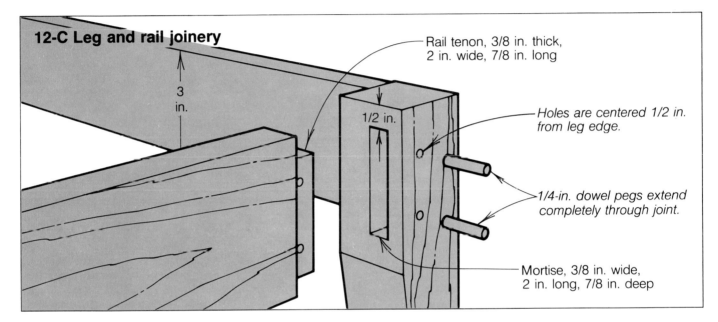

12-C Leg and rail joinery

Rail tenon, 3/8 in. thick, 2 in. wide, 7/8 in. long

3 in.

1/2 in.

Holes are centered 1/2 in. from leg edge.

1/4-in. dowel pegs extend completely through joint.

Mortise, 3/8 in. wide, 2 in. long, 7/8 in. deep

12-5 *After gluing and clamping the rails to the legs, I drill 2 holes through each joint and peg the tenons in their mortises with a pair of 1/4-in. dowels. Coat the dowels with glue before driving them, and let them protrude above the surface so that they can be sanded flush after the glue dries.*

12-6 *Strengthen the base by installing pine corner braces just inside the legs. Fasten the braces to the rails with glue and screws.*

clamp them up and peg the remaining joints (photo 12-5). To complete the base, I glue and screw corner braces in place just inside the legs (photo 12-6).

Desk cabinet: sides, frame, work surface and top

By now, your glued-up panels should be ready to cut to their finished sizes. Before you do any cutting, use a scraper to remove any hardened glue from around the joint lines. I do all the panel-cutting work on the table saw, using the rip fence and the panel cutter. To cut the sides, use the dimensions given in drawing 12-D. Cut the inner work surface 18 in. wide by 33¾ in. long. The front should measure 15⅜ in. by 30½ in. For the dimensions of the compartment dividers, see drawing 12-G.

Because my dovetail jig is set up to mill 3/8-in.-deep dovetails, the length of my top piece is 33¾ in. The top's width is trickier to calculate, since the front edge of the top has 2 bevels cut into it (see drawing 12-D). The upper bevel matches the angle of the sides' sloped fronts. The lower angle is cut at 90 degrees to the upper angle. Both of these cuts can be made on the table saw.

Now I make a pine frame for the cabinet. The frame's outside dimensions should be 18 in. by 33¾ in. All frame members are 3/4 in. thick and 2½ in. wide. The front and back members are grooved to accept 1/4-in.-thick, 1/2-in.-long tongues that are milled in the 14-in.-long side members. I mill these joints on the table saw, using the dado head (see chapter 9 for details on frame construction). When gluing and nailing the frame together, remember not to nail

12-7 Use the rip fence as a guide when milling dadoes in the desk sides. Raise the cutter 3/8 in. above the table, and adjust its width to 3/4 in.

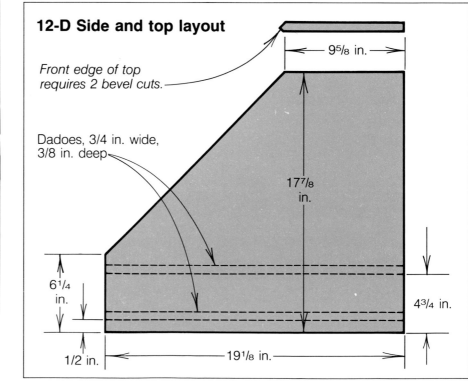

12-D Side and top layout

Front edge of top requires 2 bevel cuts.

9⅝ in.

Dadoes, 3/4 in. wide, 3/8 in. deep

17⅞ in.

6¼ in.

4¾ in.

1/2 in.

19⅛ in.

between 1¹/₈ in. and 1⁷/₈ in. from the frame end. Nails in these locations will get in the way of the dadoes you're about to cut.

The pine frame needs a pair of dadoes, which hold the divider pieces on either side of the drawer. I set up the dado head in the table saw to cut 3/4 in. wide and 1/4 in. deep. Then I position the rip fence 1³/₁₆ in. away from the cutter and run each side of the frame against the fence to cut the dadoes.

The desk sides also need dadoing. Drawing 12-D shows the dado layout. The upper dado holds the desk work surface; the lower dado holds the pine frame. I raise the cutter 3/8 in. above the table, and adjust the rip fence to guide the bottom edge of each side as I cut the dadoes (photo 12-7).

After dadoing the sides, I use the router and 3/8-in. rabbeting bit to rabbet the back edge of each side for the desk's 1/4-in.-thick plywood back. To recess the back slightly, I make this rabbet 3/8 in. wide and 3/8 in. deep. I stop the rabbet 3/8 in. from the top edge of each side so that it won't show through the top of the desk. The top of the desk can also be rabbeted now to hold the plywood back, using the same set-up on the router. Again, stop the rabbet 3/8 in. shy of either end.

Dovetailing is the next step. I set up my dovetail jig to mill the dovetail joints where the top meets the sides. My jig is just wide enough to hold the sides and the top together. The dovetail bit I use is 3/8 in. wide at its broadest point, and I carefully adjust the router so that the bit's depth of cut is also 3/8 in.

Sliding supports

I make the divider pieces next. These pieces separate the bottom drawer compartment from the sliding supports, and also control the way the supports move in and out (see drawings 12-E and 12-F). Cut from 3/4-in.-thick pine boards, the dividers are 3¹/₂ in. wide and 17¹/₂ in. long.

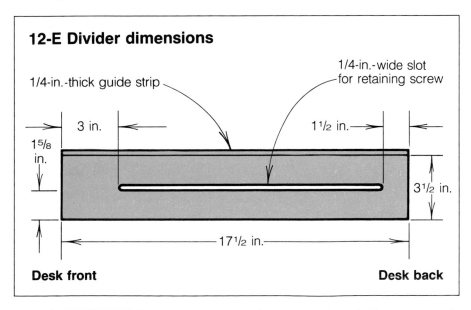

12-E Divider dimensions

1/4-in.-thick guide strip

1/4-in.-wide slot for retaining screw

3 in.

1⁵/₈ in.

1¹/₂ in.

3¹/₂ in.

17¹/₂ in.

Desk front   **Desk back**

A 1/4-in.-wide slot, located 1⅝ in. from the bottom edge of each divider, holds a screw that's driven into the support. As the support is pulled out, the screw moves along the slot, stopping 3 in. from the front edge of the divider. After cutting the dividers to their finished size, I cut the slots using a router and 1/4-in. roundnose bit. I adjust bit depth to just over 3/8 in., and make 2 plunge-cuts from both sides of the divider. The router's fence guides the bit. As shown in drawing 12-E, the slot should start 3 in. from the front of the divider, and end 1½ in. from its back edge.

When the slot is complete, I chuck a V-groove bit the the router and mill a V-shaped channel along the side of the slot that faces the drawer opening. The V-groove provides a smoother raceway for the flat-head screw, and allows you to drive the screw flush.

On top of the dividers, I screw down a 1/4-in.-thick maple guide strip. This piece is 2½ in. wide, except at the front of the desk, where it's notched out to hold the widened front section of the front support. I make this notch 13/16 in. wide and 2 in. deep.

Now it's time to glue up the parts you've been working on. Using glue and 1¼-in. drywall screws, I fasten the the dividers to the frame.

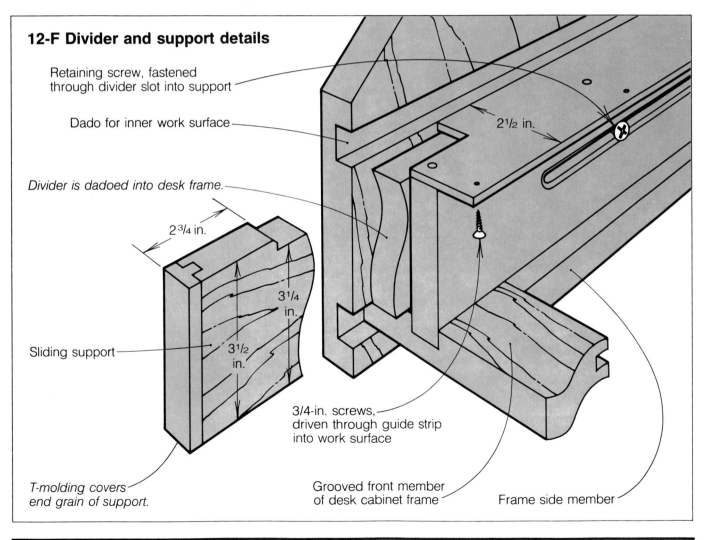

12-F Divider and support details

Retaining screw, fastened through divider slot into support

Dado for inner work surface

Divider is dadoed into desk frame.

2¾ in.

3¼ in.

3½ in.

Sliding support

T-molding covers end grain of support.

2½ in.

3/4-in. screws, driven through guide strip into work surface

Grooved front member of desk cabinet frame

Frame side member

Then I spread some glue on top of the guide strips, and glue the frame and the inner work surface to the sides. The frame and work surface should sit 3/4 in. back from the front edge of each side. I clamp up the cabinet to pull the joints tight, taking care to keep the clamps clear of the drawer opening. This way, I'll be able to make and install the sliding supports while the glue is setting. From underneath the cabinet, drive 3/4-in. screws up through the guide strips and into the work surface. To keep the assembly square until the glue sets, I set the dovetailed ends of the top loosely into their dovetailed sides.

Now for the 2 supports. These pieces are sized so that they'll slide smoothly in the housing created by the guide strip, the divider, the desk side and the frame. When closed, the supports should fit flush with the front vertical edges of the cabinet sides. These dimensions and details are shown in drawing 12-F.

The supports start out as maple boards 3/4 in. thick, 3^1/2 in. wide and 17 in. long. The front edge of each support gets special treatment in the form of a maple T-molding, glued into a groove 1/4 in. wide and 1/4 in. deep. I cut both parts of this joint on the table saw. The T-molding's shoulders are 1/2 in. thick, and its tongue is milled to match the dimensions of the groove. For safety and ease of work, I cut the T-molding as a tongue in a larger piece of wood, and then cut out the final profile.

I glue and clamp the T-molding to the front of each support. When the glue has set, I remove the clamps and use the bandsaw to cut nearly the entire support to a finished width of 3^1/4 in. Only the front 2^3/4 in. of each support remains 3^1/2 in. wide, as shown in drawing 12-F. On each support, I chamfer the 1/4-in. shoulder where the width changes. Then I test both pieces for fit and give them a thorough

12-8 Install each support by first pushing it into its fully closed position. Then drive a 1^1/4-in. drywall screw through the divider and into the support at the very back of the divider's slot.

12-9 A wood board, clamped to the desk top, guides the router as I mill stopped dadoes for the desk compartment dividers.

sanding. Finally, I install each support by driving a 1¼-in. screw through the grooved divider and into the support. Push the support all the way back in its housing, and locate the screw at the back end of the groove (photo 12-8). I pre-drill the screw holes and drive the screw just deep enough to stay clear of the V-groove.

Inside the desk

My design for the desk compartments, shown in drawing 12-G, includes 4 main vertical dividers and a row of shelves with small drawers. You might want to alter the compartment layout to suit your own needs. The joinery details can still stay the same. All the compartment dividers are cut from 1/2-in.-thick maple.

I make the 4 main vertical compartment dividers first because they're all the same size: 8½ in. wide and 12⅛ in. high, with small notches (1/4 in. deep and 3/4 in. wide) cut out of each front corner. The notches let the dividers extend just slightly beyond "stopped" dadoes that are milled in the work surface and in the underside of the desk top. The dadoes, which are 1/2 in. wide and 1/4 in. deep, extend 8 in. from the back of the desk. To mill them, I chuck a 1/2-in. mortising bit in the router, adjust its depth to 1/4 in., and clamp a wood guide board to the work surface, parallel with the dado's layout line (photo 12-9). The desk top gets the same treatment on its underside, except that there's an extra dado to hold the short vertical divider near the center of the desk. Also, the dadoes extend 8 in. from the edge of the rabbet in the top's back edge.

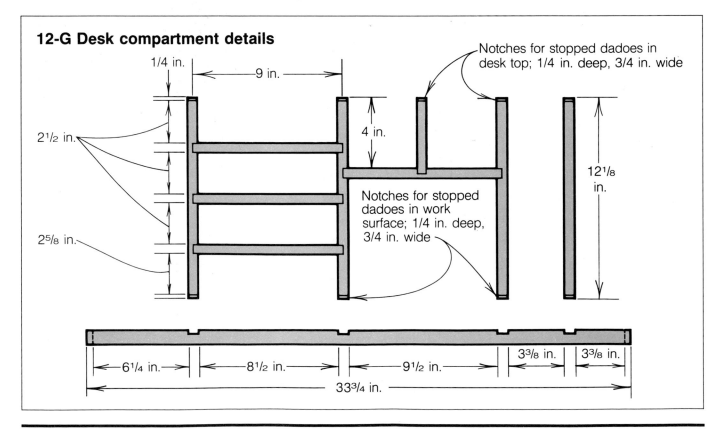

12-G Desk compartment details

Notches for stopped dadoes in desk top; 1/4 in. deep, 3/4 in. wide

Notches for stopped dadoes in work surface; 1/4 in. deep, 3/4 in. wide

1/4 in.

9 in.

4 in.

2½ in.

2⅝ in.

12⅛ in.

6¼ in. — 8½ in. — 9½ in. — 3⅜ in. — 3⅜ in.

33¾ in.

When I've finished dadoing the work surface and top, I turn to the dadoes in the vertical and horizontal pieces. These I cut on the table saw, adjusting the dado head for 1/2-in. width of cut and 1/4-in. depth of cut (photo 12-10). As you complete the compartment assembly, test-fit all the parts together and make sure that the dadoes in the top will fit down over all the vertical pieces at the same time that the top's dovetailed ends mate with the sides.

If everything fits, take the entire assembly apart and give the back of the inner work surface and all the dividers a final sanding. Once the compartments are in place, you won't be able to sand them or the work surface effectively.

Finally it's time to glue up the rest of the cabinet (photo 12-11). Applying the glue carefully with a small brush, I first assemble the center shelves and the three vertical dividers that support them. If necessary, the solitary divider and the short vertical divider can actually be slid into their dadoes after the top has been installed. I dab the dovetails with glue and drive the joints together with my shot-filled mallet. Use clamps as necessary to pull all the joints tight.

12-10 Dadoes for the horizontal dividers are cut on the table saw, with the rip fence used as a guide.

Drawer and front construction

The 3 small drawers that fit inside the desk are all the same size. These drawers are meant to be pulled out frequently, so they shouldn't fit too tightly. The sides of my drawers are pine, 1/2 in. thick, 2³/₈

12-11 Vertical compartment dividers are glued into their dadoes in the work surface. The desk top will then be glued into the sides and over the vertical dividers.

in. wide and 8³/₈ in. long. Drawer fronts are identical in thickness, width and length, but they're made from maple. I use 1/4-in. plywood for the drawer bottoms and 1/2-in. pine for the backs.

After cutting all the drawer parts to size, I clamp up the fronts and sides in my dovetail jig and mill dovetail joints where these parts join. I set up the jig so that the dovetails show in the drawer sides. Then I run the sides and fronts through the dado cutter on the table saw to cut the dadoes for the drawer bottoms. These dadoes are 1/4 in. wide, 1/4 in. deep, and located 1/4 in. from the bottom edge of each side and front. Finally, I adjust the dado for a 1/2-in.-wide cut, and dado the sides to accept the backs. Thanks to the dovetail jig and dado cutter, it doesn't take me long to produce 3 small, identical drawers for inside the desk (photo 12-12).

Before you begin making the large drawer, a small face frame needs to be installed at the front of the desk. This 4-piece, 3/4-in.-thick frame covers the edges of the work surface, the front frame member and the divider pieces. The face frame's 2 horizontal pieces, or rails, also fit into the dadoes in the sides, as shown in photo 12-13. The top rail is 1 in. wide, except for 1¹⁵/₁₆-in.-long notches at either end. Notch depth is 1/4 in. The bottom rail is 1¹/₄ in. wide, except where it's notched to fit into the bottom dadoes in the sides.

I build the desk's large drawer just as I build the drawers in the chest of drawers project (chapter 9). The 3/4-in.-thick drawer front is rabbeted (3/8 in. deep and 3/8 in. wide) to overlay its opening on the top and sides. I dovetail the sides into the front, then mill a 1/4-in. bead on all 4 edges of the drawer front. If you haven't built a drawer like this before, study the text and step-by-step photos in chapter 9.

12-12 Each small drawer for inside the desk has its sides dovetailed into its front. After gluing sides and front together, I slide in the bottom before gluing and nailing the back in place.

12-13 A narrow face frame is glued around the large drawer opening and the sliding supports. The ends of the face frame rails fit into dadoes in the sides of the desk cabinet.

The finished size of the front is 15³/₈ in. by 33³/₄ in. The long dimension includes a pair of breadboard edges, which cover the endgrain of the boards with a hidden tongue-and-groove joint. These edge pieces are 2 in. wide and 15³/₈ in. long.

To mill the groove in the breadboard edges, I use a 1/4-in. slot-cutting bit in the router. This bit has a pilot bearing, and will make a groove that's 1/4 in. wide and 3/8 in. deep. I adjust the router so that the slot is centered exactly along the edge of the stock. Then with the edge piece clamped on the workbench, I start and finish the slot about 1/4 in. from each end.

The glued-up panel for the front has to be cut down to a finished size of 15³/₈ in. by 32¹/₂ in. When this is done, you can mill the tongues along the end-grain edges (photo 12-14). I switch to a rabbeting bit in the router for this job. Use a bit with a pilot bearing that will let the cutter penetrate 3/8 in. into the stock. Adjust the router so that after 2 passes along each edge, a 1/4-in.-thick tongue will remain.

At each corner of the panel, you'll have to trim off a small triangle of the tongue so that the edge pieces will fit. I use a back saw to cut off these pieces, and smooth the resulting shoulders with a chisel. When you get a tight fit at the corners, glue and clamp the breadboard edges to the front (photo 12-15).

As soon as the glue dries, the front can be finished off. The first step is to rabbet the inside edges along the top and sides of the piece. The rabbet allows the front to overlay the desk sides and top by 3/8 in. Unlike a conventional rabbet, this one has a shoulder that's angled 22 degrees to create a more comfortable work surface when the front

12-14 I mill a tongue along the end-grain edges of the front, using a router and 3/8-in. rabbeting bit. Adjust bit depth so that after 2 passes, a 1/4-in.-thick tongue remains.

12-15 The corners of the tongue need to be trimmed to fit the groove milled in the breadboard edge. When a test-fit shows a tight joint, I glue and clamp the edges to the panel.

12-16 *To mill the angled rabbet along the front's side and top edges, I use a 22-degree laminate-trim bit with its bearing removed and its lower shank filed off. I mill the rabbet in several passes, adjusting both the router fence and the bit depth after each pass.*

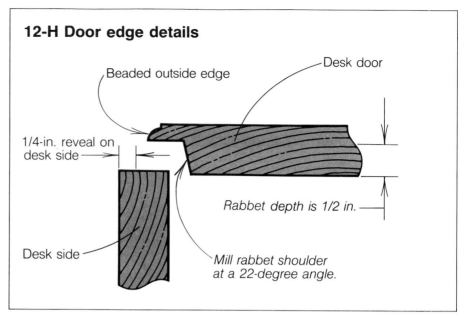

12-H Door edge details

Beaded outside edge

Desk door

1/4-in. reveal on desk side

Rabbet depth is 1/2 in.

Desk side

Mill rabbet shoulder at a 22-degree angle.

is open (see drawing 12-H). It took me a while to figure out how to mill this unusual beveled rabbet. The solution is a 22-degree laminate-trim bit. This bit comes with a bearing, mounted on a shank that extends below the carbide-tipped cutters. I detach the bearing, then cut the shank off with a fine-toothed hacksaw and file it flush with the bottom of the cutters. Then I chuck the bit in my router and attach the router's fence.

To avoid straining the router and overheating both the bit and the wood, I mill the rabbet in several stages (photo 12-16). After each pass around the top and sides, I adjust the fence and the bit depth to cut a little deeper and a little wider. At each setting, it's important to make your first pass along the top edge, so you can finish by milling with the grain of the breadboard edges. The work is done when rabbet depth and width both equal 1/2 in.

All 4 outside edges of the front can now be beaded. I did this with the router, using a 1/4-in. roundover bit and a fence attached to the router. The fence controls the width of the cut, since the rabbets leave nothing for the bit's bearing to ride against. I adjust the fence and the depth of cut so that the bit leaves a 1/16-in. shoulder at the top of the curved edge. Another way to bead the front is to use the 1/4-in. roundover bit in the router table.

The back of the desk cabinet is fairly easy to attach. First, I complete the rabbet to hold the back by squaring up its corners, where the sides meet the desk top. Use a sharp chisel for this work. The back itself is 1/4-in.-thick, maple-veneered plywood. A size of 18 1/4 in. by 33 3/4 in. should fit the rabbeted sides and top and extend down to the bottom of the cabinet. I use glue and 3/4-in. drywall screws (in pre-drilled holes) to install the panel.

Since this is such a traditional piece, I use a pair of thick brass butt hinges to join the front to the inner work surface. The hinges should be mortised into both surfaces. You can do this by hand, with a sharp utility knife and a chisel (see chapter 6, photos 6-7 and 6-8), or use a router with a mortising bit and jig. Either way, install the hinges on the front first, then center the front on the sides to locate the exact hinge position.

I use a total of 8 Shaker knobs on this desk: 3 for the small drawers, 2 for the large drawer (located directly below the hinges), 1 for the front and 1 for each sliding support. My knobs are turned from maple, with a diameter of 3/4 in. Each knob has a 1/4-in.-diameter pin protruding from its bottom. To install the knobs, you have to drill out for the pin and then glue the knob in the hole.

If you haven't done so already, it's time to join the desk cabinet to its base. The cabinet is sized to rest on the tops of the legs. I make sure the cabinet is centered, then drive a single screw through each corner brace and into the pine frame of the cabinet. To create an attractive transition where base and cabinet meet, I install a small cove molding around the front and sides. The molding covers the rail edges that are exposed with the cabinet in place.

Because I couldn't find a maple cove molding in the right size, I made my own, using a 1/2-in. cove-molding bit in the router table. Starting with a piece of maple 5/8 in. thick and 1 3/8 in. wide, I mill a cove along 2 edges, and then simply rip the stock in half, lengthwise, on the table saw. The 3 pieces of molding are mitered where they join at the front corners of the desk. After pre-drilling the holes, I fasten the molding to the rails with glue and 3/4-in. brads (photo 12-17). When you install the molding, be sure not to nail or glue the molding to the cabinet, since this will make it impossible to break the desk down into its 2 major parts.

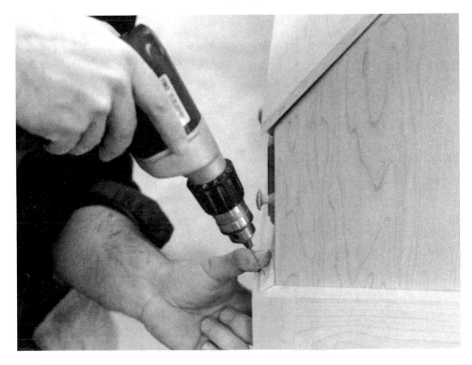

12-17 I install a small maple cove molding at the juncture of cabinet and base. Side pieces are mitered to the front piece. To avoid splitting the molding, pre-drill the nail holes. Glue and nail the molding to the base only, so that the desk cabinet can be lifted free if you need to move the entire desk.

Chapter 13

Finishing

$\mathbf{I}$n a woodworker's vocabulary, the term "finish" can mean anything from a simple application of paste wax or tung oil to multiple coats of sealer, stain, varnish or even paint. Whatever the treatment, the purpose is always the same: to protect and beautify the wood. In this chapter, I'll describe some popular finishes and show you how to apply them. But first, we need to spend some time preparing the wood for whatever finish it will get.

Surface preparation

A great finishing job starts with the wood itself. The smoother the wood, the better the finish will look. This is especially true if you plan to use a light stain or a clear finish. These finishes will actually highlight scratches, holes and other irregularities in the wood surface.

Holes left from setting finishing nails will need to be filled at some point in the finishing process. Some woodworkers like to fill these holes prior to final sanding, but my preference is to wait until after the finish has been applied to fill them. Using different shades of wood putty, I can custom-mix the wood putty to duplicate the exact shade of the finish. With a painted finish, I fill nail holes with glazing compound before applying the final coat of paint.

Small voids that remain when joints are glued together can usually be filled even before the glue dries. Working right over the hole, I dust some sawdust onto a small amount of glue, mixing up a paste to dab into the hole (photo 13-1). When this shop-made wood filler has dried, you can sand it flush.

Compared to the challenge of actually building a piece of furniture, sanding isn't much fun. But it's crucial for a good finish. Fortunately, there are some simple ways to cut down on sanding time without compromising the smooth surface you need to produce. The first step is to do plenty of preliminary sanding as you're building the piece of furniture. Once the piece has been assembled, many parts are more difficult to sand evenly because corners and edges become difficult to

13-1 To fill small voids in a joint, you can make your own wood filler with glue and fine sawdust. Be sure the sawdust comes from the same species of wood you're filling.

reach. So give these pieces their final sanding while they're still apart.

One of the best ways to speed "surface prep" is use the right abrasive grit and the right sanding tool at the right time. The grit designation given to sandpaper refers to the size of the abrasive particles that are bonded to a paper or cloth backing. It's the minute sharp edges on these particles that actually scrape the wood surface, producing sawdust. The larger the abrasive particles, the coarser the grit. As shown in the chart, the coarsest grits have the lowest grit numbers.

I don't use coarse-grit sandpaper on any new furniture projects. Coarse particles are large enough to leave gouges in bare wood that take time to remove with finer grits. On the other hand, it's also unwise to start sanding with paper that's too fine. I base my grit choice on the hardness of the wood and how much wood I want to remove. In most cases, I start out with medium-grit for the preliminary sanding. Then I switch to fine-grit paper. Finally, table tops and other parts that need an extra level of smoothness are sanded with either 180-grit or 220-grit paper.

Sandpaper varies not just by grit, but also by the type of abrasive particles that are used. I prefer aluminum oxide abrasive over garnet and flint. The latter 2 abrasives don't hold their sharpness as long; and tend to "load up," or trap wood fibers between abrasive particles.

Whenever possible, I use portable electric sanders in favor of sanding by hand. It's a lot faster. The belt sander is good for

Sandpaper grits and recommended uses

Grit#	Category	Common uses
36 40 50 60	Coarse	Refinishing floors, removing paint
80 100	Medium	Preliminary sanding, shaping and smoothing of bare wood
120 150	Fine	Final sanding on bare wood
180 220 240	Very fine	Final sanding for a super-smooth surface on bare wood; sanding between coats of paint or varnish
280 320	Extra fine	Sanding between coats of paint or varnish

smoothing large, flat areas like table tops, or whenever quite a bit of wood must be removed. In photo 13-2, I'm belt-sanding the medicine cabinet (chapter 1) to smooth the finger-jointed corners flush with the side of the cabinet case.

An orbital sander (also called a pad sander or finishing sander) is the tool to use for final sanding (photo 13-3). In addition to going over flat surfaces with the orbital sander, I give all edges and corners a quick hit by hand to soften them. My sander is a "quarter-sheet" model designed to hold 1/4 of a 9x11 sheet of sandpaper. But it's more economical for me to buy sandpaper in long rolls. These 4 1/2-in.-wide rolls are available in different grits from building supply outlets and mail-order suppliers.

When I've finished sanding a piece, I spend a few minutes brushing off the sawdust that's accumulated on the wood surfaces. On large pieces, a shop vacuum with a brush attachment makes quick work of this operation.

13-2 The belt sander works best in situations where quite a bit of wood needs to be removed on a flat area. It's meant to be used with both hands.

13-3 This small orbital sander can be used with one hand. It's ideal for delicate smoothing operations like the final sanding before assembling a joint or applying finish.

Paint, stain and polyurethane

Now is the time to move your piece of furniture into a separate room. Workshops are simply too dusty for applying finish. Ideally, you want dry-to-average humidity, comfortable temperature, very little dust and good ventilation. In terms of standard equipment, a pair of coveralls is a good idea, or at least an old shirt and an old pair of pants. Keep a good supply of clean rags on hand, as well as clean containers in different sizes for applying finish and soaking brushes.

Before any finish is applied, I give the wood a final wipe-down with a tack rag. Impregnated with just enough varnish to make it sticky, the tack rag does a good job of picking up minute sawdust particles that have worked their way into the pores of the wood. You can make your own tack rags, or buy them, ready-to-use, at the hardware or paint store. Get the wood as clean as you can, because any dust that remains will get in the way of an even finish.

No matter what finish you apply, it's best not to work straight from the can of finish unless you know you'll be completely using up the contents. By transferring a smaller amount of paint, stain or varnish into a clean container for application, you avoid contaminating leftover finish with lint, sawdust or brush bristles.

If I want a clear, durable finish on a piece of furniture (on the blanket chest, for example), I use a high-quality polyurethane varnish, in either gloss or satin. Compared to the old-fashioned spar varnishes, polyurethane is easier to apply and at least as durable. You can apply most polyurethanes directly over bare wood, or over wood that's been stained with a compatible stain.

I often use sanding sealer as a base coat beneath one or more coats of polyurethane. Sanding sealer is clear, quick-drying and less expensive than polyurethane. It's formulated so that it can be sanded easily (after it dries) to provide a super-smooth base for polyurethane or paint. Sanding sealer is also good to use as an overall sealer on areas that won't be seen, like the undersides of table tops and the insides of drawers. Remember that both sides and all exposed edges of a board need to be sealed to prevent the uneven absorption of moisture, which can cause warping. After the sanding sealer has dried, I sand all areas that will receive polyurethane, using extra-fine-grit sandpaper.

To apply polyurethane, use straight, even strokes, brushing with the grain of the wood. Avoid going over finish that you've already applied, and don't shake or vigorously stir the finish because this will cause bubbles that can remain in the finish after it dries. If you want to apply additional coats, follow the manufacturer's directions.

Penetrating finishes also fall into the category of clear finishes, but they're meant to penetrate into the pores of the wood rather than cover the wood surface. The candle stand has a penetrating finish that does a good job of showing off the rich tone of its cherry wood. Penetrating finishes are easy to apply because the technique is to flood the wood surface with finish and then wipe away any residue that isn't absorbed and remains on the wood surface. Hardness, stain-resistance and luster are built up after several applications.

Paint requires the same surface preparation and application techniques used for polyurethane. Instead of a clear sanding sealer base coat, I often use a quick-drying primer. Quite a few paint manufacturers offer colors that closely match the traditional hues used in Colonial times. If you can't find the right stock color, most paint stores will custom-mix a color for you.

Stains are also formulated to simulate the look of antique wood. But a stain's effect is less predictable, since wood species and grain characteristics determine how a piece of wood will absorb stain. Application technique is also a factor. If you brush stain on liberally and allow it to sit for 10 minutes before wiping down the surface, you'll maximize the amount of pigment that stays in the wood. On the other hand, wiping the stain on with a clean cloth allows you to limit the pigmentation for a subtler effect. The end grain of any board will always absorb more stain that the face or edge grain, so end-grain applications should always be carefully done.

Because stain can have such a varying effect, I always test-finish some scrap stock before actually staining the furniture. The scrap wood should come from the same boards you use to make the furniture. If uneven stain absorption seems to be a problem, I can apply a pre-stain sealer to selected areas in order to control the effect of the stain. One or more trial-runs through the staining process ensure that there won't be any surprises when you finish the furniture.

Once stain has been applied and allowed to dry, I like to give the wood 2 coats of satin polyurethane. This seals the wood surface and makes it easy to wipe clean with a damp towel.

THE NEW YANKEE WORKSHOP

Norm Abram has become known as the most famous carpenter since Joseph on the PBS television series *This Old House*. He's the master craftsman whose legendary woodworking skills, ingenuity, and inspired teaching have guided millions of viewers through the hands-on process of home renovation. In his new series, Norm invites you into his "New Yankee Workshop" as he turns his woodworking prowess to the practical art of building traditional-style furniture. This volume, the companion to the television series, takes you step-by-step with Norm as he constructs handsome and useful pieces for the home, including a medicine cabinet, drop-leaf table, blanket chest, bedside table, bathroom vanity, trestle table, bookshelf, chest of drawers, candle stand, hutch, and writing desk.

Craftsmen in earlier days did all their work by hand, cutting joints and straightening wood with sharp saws, chisels, and hand planes. Their skills took years to master, and the results live on in treasured heirlooms. In *The New Yankee Workshop,* Norm demonstrates how you can practice these time-honored cabinetmaking techniques by combining the greater speed and accuracy of power tools with basic woodworking experience.

The furniture from Norm's workshop features the simple lines, pleasing proportions, and superb mortise-and-tenon joinery inspired by classic Shaker designs. Norm gives detailed, step-at-a-time instructions for every project,